# THE GOLDIE EFFECT

## HOW TO REWRITE YOUR LIFE WITHOUT BURNING IT DOWN

## MICHELLE HOOEY

This book reflects the author's personal experiences and perspectives and is not intended to provide medical, psychological, legal, or professional advice. Readers are encouraged to consult appropriate professionals regarding their individual circumstances.

ISBN 978-1-0673741-0-5 (Paperback)

ISBN 978-1-0673741-1-2 (eBook)

Published by: Michelle Hooey

anchorlesscoaching.com

Printed in Canada

First Edition

Cover design by: Elle Jackson

Interior design by: Taryn Nergaard

Edited by: Alethea Spiridon

# PRAISE FOR THE GOLDIE EFFECT

"Michelle writes with a depth of honesty and compassion that instantly makes you feel less alone. *The Goldie Effect* is a powerful reminder that we don't need to avoid hard things to live a beautiful life. All we need is the right support to move through them."

—COURTNEY THOMAS, FOUNDER
OF THE BODHI EFFECT

"*The Goldie Effect* is a deeply personal story of pain and perseverance, told with the kind of unapologetic honesty only found in someone who's been through the fire and lived to tell the tale. Michelle writes from inside a complex medical journey, and from the profound lessons she earned along the way, generously shaping her lived experience into something readers can hold. This book is for the resilient mother in all of us, and for anyone searching for grounded wisdom on the far side of grief."

—ANNA MULLENS, AWARD-WINNING
PRODUCER, STORYTELLER, & INTERNATIONAL
COMMUNICATIONS EXECUTIVE

"*The Goldie Effect* is powerful, activating, and deeply nourishing. From the first pages, you feel Goldie's fierce, embodied energy. It's tangible, motivating, and keeps you turning the pages. I loved the balance between strength and comfort. The guidance sections at the end are beautifully organized and practical, making it easy to revisit and integrate the wisdom. This is a book you'll want to read more than once. An inspiring read for anyone interested in healing and stepping into their inner strength. Highly recommend."

—KRISTINA CAVALLARI, NERVOUS
SYSTEM GUIDE + FOUNDER

"*The Goldie Effect* is Michelle's deeply personal tale of her experience getting to know her daughter, Goldie, who has complex medical needs. Michelle tells the story of how Goldie taught her to shift, move, and adapt to her circumstances, which began to create powerful changes in her life. If you want to read an inspiring story of love, connection, change, and growth, *The Goldie Effect* is for you."

—JULIE PETERS, AUTHOR OF MAIDEN,
WARRIOR, MOTHER, CRONE

"Michelle writes with unflinching honesty about living a life she didn't choose with a medically complex child, offering insight into how she keeps herself grounded even on the hardest days. She captures the brutal collision of grief and joy, tender mothering, and relentless medical advocacy. Despite her deep fears, she is defiantly hopeful and has always refused to accept the limits placed on her child. This story is devastating, heartwarming, complicated, and hopeful."

—MEL ZEE, WRITER + MEDIA CREATOR
(AND GOLDIE'S AUNT)

"*The Goldie Effect* feels like a real human connection. As someone who works every day with bodies, nervous systems, and the stories we carry, I felt the truth of Michelle's experiences immediately. She weaves her own story with such honesty and care that I didn't want to end the conversation or put the book down. Weaving lived experience with practical tools (the 15-Minute Reset) feels like having a supportive conversation with a friend, one who can lovingly share wisdom and care. I didn't finish this book feeling like I needed to fix myself; I finished it feeling steadier, more seen, and reminded that real transformation happens through small, consistent moments of presence and connections. Pour a cup of tea and dive right in, you won't regret it."

—LAURA KIELEY, FOUNDER OF THE PRACTICE

"From the very first page, *The Goldie Effect* captivates you, pulling you into a raw, real experience that feels both deeply personal and wildly expansive. It's the kind of page-turner you don't just read, but you feel in your soul. Prepare to cry and come out on the other side of this book a different person."

—MEGAN REED, BESTSELLING AUTHOR + COACH

"I expected a memoir about an unbearably hard season. What I found was something far more generous and useful. *The Goldie Effect* doesn't stay in the story of suffering; it guides you through how to live with clarity, presence, and meaning in the middle of chaos. The wisdom here is both profound and practical, honouring the depth of real trauma while offering tools you can use. This is a book I will return to repeatedly."

— JEN STEWART, ANAT BANIEL METHOD®
NEUROMOVEMENT PRACTITIONER

For my little loves, Frankie and Goldie—
my greatest teachers, and the reason I became a mama.

For my big love, Jeff—
my ride or die, the one who stands beside me through
every pivot, every wild idea.

And for every human "in it" right now—
I'm sending so much love your way.

# CONTEXT

# INTRODUCTION

**YOU NEVER KNOW THE MOMENT YOUR LIFE WILL SPLIT IN** two—before and after—until it's staring you straight in the eyes. For me, that moment was **March 10, 2023,** the day my daughter, Goldie, came into the world and refused to breathe.

A diagnosis, a phone call, a birth, any of them can turn everything you thought you knew into smoke. For me, it was all three. What followed were five months that stripped me bare and rebuilt me, teaching me what resilience, faith, and surrender mean.

This isn't just the story of a mother and her medically complex child. It's a story about finding your way when life cracks you open, about learning to trust yourself again when control is gone. This book is the deeply personal story of navigating life with a child whose medical needs rewrote everything I thought I knew.

It started as Goldie's story, but as I lived it, I realized it was something bigger. Most people don't truly start living until something forces them to wake up. The Goldie Effect is about that awakening: the moment you stop abandoning yourself and start listening to the truth you've been carrying all along. It's for the moment you know something must change, but you don't know what the next step is.

Inside, you'll find grounded tools and lived experience. The things that helped me rebuild myself when everything fell apart. You'll meet the Fifteen-Minute Rewrite, born in those 2 a.m. hospital rooms when fifteen minutes was all I had. It's designed to cut through overwhelm and rebuild your life in sustainable micro-moments. Take your time with this book. Let it meet you where you are.

The Goldie Effect is the spark. The Rewrite is the deeper work. Together, they are everything. This book starts out in the fire because I want you to feel where we were in the journey.

The Goldie Effect is living inside uncertainty without losing yourself.

It's a guide to rewriting your life when the one you're living no longer feels like yours. It's for the moments when you wake up and realize you've been surviving instead of living, following rules you never agreed to, carrying weight that was never meant to be yours, and abandoning who you are just to make it through the day.

You don't need a crisis to earn a rewrite. You don't need tragedy to prove you're allowed to want more. And if you *have* walked through the fire, if grief, trauma, or fear are still humming under your skin, this book will meet you right there, without pretending any of it is easy.

This book is a path out of being stuck, out of self-abandonment. Not a checklist but a way back to yourself. A living, breathing process built from what saved me, and what will help you rewrite the life you're into one that actually fits.

I invite you to be gentle with yourself as you move through this book. Let the stories meet you where you are. Buckle up. There will be tears. There will be miracles.

There will be moments that knock the wind out of you, and moments that put it back.

## THE PROMISE OF THE GOLDIE EFFECT

The Goldie Effect is divine trust in motion.
The quiet decision to keep choosing yourself, even when the path is unclear.

It's finding your way through uncertainty without abandoning who you are.

You're not doing this alone.
You're more held than you think, more loved than you know, and stronger than you feel, even on the days it doesn't feel true.

This may not be easy.
But this book isn't asking you to overhaul your life or become someone else.
It's the heartbeat of the 15-Minute Rewrite, a way of coming back to yourself slowly, gently, sustainably, when everything feels loud or fragile or unfinished.

At the end of each chapter, you'll find a 15-Minute Rewrite invitation.
Because in the beginning, fifteen minutes was all I had.
And repeatedly it proved to be enough.

You don't have to rush.
You don't have to get it right.
You just have to stay.

Ready?
Let's step into the fire.

# BEFORE THE FIRE

BEFORE ALL OF THIS, I WAS IN CONSTANT MOTION. PLANES, projects, new cities, new stories. Ten years spent working across continents, chasing adventure like oxygen. Work hard, play hard was my motto, and I meant it. My passport was full, my calendar was fuller, and I wore "busy" like a badge of honour.

Adventure was my love language long before I met Jeff. When we fell in love, we built our life around that same wide-eyed wonder. Weekend ferry rides with our Labradoodles, spontaneous day trips, and tropical escapes with Frankie, my eldest daughter, in tow. Movement felt like proof we were doing life right.

At home, our mornings were joyful chaos, coffee brewing, dogs underfoot, Frankie dancing in her pajamas while I responded to emails from my phone. I worked in tech, juggling deadlines and dreams, convinced that "balance" was just another thing I could master.

We were happy, busy, building, always reaching for the next thing, the next project, the next trip, the next milestone. If you'd asked me then, I would've said I was thriving. But underneath, I was sprinting. My nervous system didn't know what rest felt like. My worth was measured in doing, not being.

I didn't know it yet, but everything I thought I was the achiever, the traveler, the woman who could handle it all—was about to burn away. The woman who lived on ambition, and constant motion was about to go still.

# THE
# FIRE

*Part 1*

# BURN TO BEGIN

"Your mind is fire. It can heat your house or burn it to the ground."

— **BRIANNA WIEST,** *SALT WATER*

THE MOMENT GOLDIE ARRIVED, EVERYTHING I THOUGHT was solid gave way. This is where the fire first touched my life. Quiet, searing, impossible to ignore.

When I read the Brianna Wiest quote, I stopped breathing for a second because I knew it was true. Not in theory, in my body. Nothing brought that fire into focus faster than my daughter, Goldie.

Let me tell you about her.

Goldie was born with brain stem dysfunction, the part of the brain that controls every vital function: breathing, swallowing, coughing, blinking. When she was born, she didn't do any of it. The doctors told us she likely never would. The room was small, the lighting awful, the air thick. The moment the doctor said, "Irregular MRI," my chest caved in.

At first, they thought it might be an oxygen injury, something that happened during birth. But later, they ruled that out. If it had been, she wouldn't have developed the reflexes she has now. Goldie's brain, the one they said was too damaged, is learning. It's rewiring. She's doing things they told us were impossible. She learned to blink. She learned to cough. She learned to breathe on her own.

Watching her brain fight to learn the basics of being alive forced me to rethink everything I believed about change. If her brain could learn to breathe, maybe mine could learn something too. My heart started to soften; maybe I wasn't as stuck as I thought.

The brain is always building something, sometimes in ways we can't see until we're ready. I learned that watching Goldie's body learn how to breathe. It's not just mindset. It's neuroplasticity. It's science and heart, and it's available to you, starting now. You don't have to have it all figured out, but you do get to believe that something new is possible. That belief is the first rewrite. The rest will follow.

When Goldie was born, everything I thought I knew about control, planning, and personal power shattered. I'd done the work — the journaling, the visualizing, the meditating and none of it meant a thing when I saw my daughter come into the world fighting for her life. I felt myself pulled between fear and trust. I chose to rewire not just my mindset, but my entire nervous system.

I used to think control looked like colour-coded calendars and a life I could organize into neat little boxes. I built a whole identity out of schedules and structure. But none of that mattered in the hospital room. There's no spreadsheet for the moment your child doesn't breathe on her own. No system that can hold you steady when the ground gives out.

Goldie forced my mind to surrender the illusion of control. Nothing about her arrival matched the life I had pictured. Everything I believed about myself, my power, and my life was thrown into the fire. I didn't know what would come next. I only knew there was no going back.

# WHEN LIFE CRACKS YOU OPEN

"Darkness is doing
its divine job."

— KRISTEN L. HARPER

 you think you can give. Loss, fear, and uncertainty became the air I breathed. This is where everything I thought I knew began to fall away.

## EMPTY SAC

The day before everything changed.

The empty sac.

I just kept repeating the same two things over and over in my head: Multiple losses.

Empty sac.

I feel like an empty sac. So scared for tomorrow. So scared to try again.

I know I'm brave and strong but not today.

Today, I am an empty sac.

Tomorrow is a new day. A harder one. But tomorrow I will no longer be an empty sac.

I will be going through a loss. I will be starting a new beginning.


The weight of that loss felt heavy beyond words, like I was sinking and couldn't find the surface. I needed somewhere to land, somewhere my body could breathe again. That's how I found myself on Cortes Island.

On a warm day in August 2021, I was swimming in a

green, clear lake on a remote island in the wild Pacific Northwest. Cortes Island is a magical island. A few of my most favourite humans moved there and lived in tiny homes on land where they grew their own food, raised chickens and goats. Swam naked in the sea and embraced their wild. I loved going there; it was an escape from my busy city life. Slow morning coffee, nothing to do but connect, make art, tend to the garden. Live the dream.

The lake on this particular day was quiet. You must trespass to get there and jump in off an old dock. We were the only ones there, me and my two goddess friends who lived there. We laughed; we swam. We soaked up the warm sun on our topless bodies. I felt so free, so alive, so perfectly content in that moment. Every dive into the green lake felt like a rebirth, spiritual in nature. I remember thinking this place was magic, and the moment was perfect. You know those moments where you pause and realize you'll never forget it.

In that quiet green water, something in me shifted. I didn't understand it then, but that lake became the place I returned to when everything else felt too heavy to hold. Inside, something small was waking up, even as everything around me felt like it was collapsing.

Every time I dove under that cold green water, my body softened. The moss, the breath, the stillness — it was my first real taste of safety, long before I knew it was also rewiring me.

I flew home to the suburbs of Vancouver a few days later, my hair salty and tangled in tight French-braid pigtails.

My daughter, Frankie, was so young. It was one of my first trips away as a mom. I felt like "me" again after returning.

And as life always does, the magic of that moment didn't stop the hard moments from coming. It just gave me somewhere to return to when it did.

Those days were hard. Jeff, my husband, and I were trying for a second child which felt like for years at that point but was probably only months. I was incredibly impatient and excited with the idea of a sibling for Frankie. We struggled. Loss after loss, it was heartbreaking. We saw specialists, ran tests. I was "perfectly healthy," so was Jeff. We kept trying.

It was exhausting. Sex when trying to conceive, especially after losses, is *not sexy*. It's a mission. I was sad. I started working with a healer and talking about my womb space. Trying to feel more connected to it. Trying to convince my own body that it was still a safe place to grow a baby. She guided me through a visualization of my womb and what it would look like. How I would enter my womb space so I could go get comfortable there, visit the spirit trying to come to me. The entrance came to me in seconds.

The green lake on Cortes Island.

The divine feminine energy was palpable that day and was perfect. Whenever I wanted to visit my womb space, I'd dive under that green water in my mind and land in the mossy quiet place that had become my refuge.

My spirit baby was a little light, scared to come into the world. I tried to comfort them; tell them it would be okay. They would be safe. I even visualized Frankie and Jeff coming to visit this little spirit. It helped me process the losses. I'd visit this lake and dive in whenever I wanted to connect and see how my spirit baby was doing. Sometimes playful, mostly scared. I know now why it was sacred, but at the time I didn't understand. I kept telling them we would love them and take care of them, and we will have a beautiful life. But take your time and come when you're ready, even though I knew I couldn't take many more losses and the "trying" was getting hard.

Those dives, real and imagined, became small places to breathe again, flickers of belief inside all the grief. Little moments where I let myself believe in something bigger than the grief in front of me. I didn't realize yet how much I'd need that belief.

We got a second dog in the midst of all the losses. He was our "COVID baby" but the truth was he was my emotional support dog. Pregnancy losses break you quietly. You attach fast, long before it feels logical. Artie was my saviour in a lot of ways. He knew exactly what to do when I wept for these little lights, my babies. He laid on my lap as long as I needed.

By that point, the grief was layered. Loss on top of loss. Hope on top of fear. It was wearing me down and waking me up at the same time.

Five pregnancy losses later. On another visit to Cortes Island, I was doing some soul searching on a rowboat in the middle of the ocean between islands when my phone started to ring. Shocked to have reception, I fumbled to answer it; it was our family doctor calling on a Saturday afternoon. It was about Frankie. Her blood work revealed she was celiac. The doctor said, "Frankie needs to stop eating gluten immediately."

The call ended. The ocean kept rocking the rowboat. And I stopped eating gluten too.

The next month, in a haze at a friend's wedding, I felt a little weird and took a test. It was a faint pink line. I didn't want to get my hopes up, but decided to pee on another stick at a truck stop on our way home. A long drive through the mountains. I wanted to tell Jeff right away.

I decided to wait in case the baby didn't stick. I told Jeff a few days later, and we were both excited but nervous. The first couple of weeks were tough, constantly peeing on sticks, going to get my HcG bloodwork checked and then at six weeks I woke up and went to the bathroom, and there was blood in my panties. We called the doctor, and they said I could get an ultrasound early based on my history with pregnancy losses. I was devastated. Then the blood stopped. My HcG wasn't going down, and we went in for an ultrasound, and our baby was there with a heartbeat. I had a subchorionic hematoma.

When the baby implants, sometimes it can cause a blood clot, which can increase the risk of miscarriage. I was told to take it easy for the remainder of my pregnancy. It was still early in the pregnancy, and I was already scared and tiptoeing around. Now I was terrified. For the next ten weeks, I had regular checkups and at sixteen weeks, it was determined I was in the clear.

Baby was bigger than the hematoma and looked healthy. For the remainder of my pregnancy, it was considered normal; baby and I were both healthy. I was so relieved.

So much so, we planned a babymoon/anniversary trip out of the country!

We booked a trip to Palm Springs, just Jeff and me, at about twenty-eight weeks. It was magical. Swimming in the pool, feeling comfortable for the first time in pregnancy since I was high risk with Frankie, finally in the clear. I knew from early on in my heart that this baby would be fine. Even those first ten weeks when the doctors weren't sure, I was.

We ate delicious food, went swimming, hiked, drove around and checked out all the amazing architecture. It was perfect. At the Palm Springs airport, if you've never been, it's open-air and chill. We were waiting for our flight, stretched out on the fake grass, looking up at the palm trees, thinking every airport should feel this easy. Then my phone buzzed. A text from my mom.

I knew right away something was wrong.

"Are you still in Palm Springs? I need to talk to you when you're home."

I called immediately. I couldn't wait through the two-hour flight. She answered and told me she had stage-two squamous cell carcinoma.

Skin cancer. WTF.

They were going to start her with radiation treatments right away. They wanted to treat it aggressively with six weeks of treatment daily. My head was spinning. I was on my babymoon, finally feeling safe in this pregnancy and now my mom had cancer. My mom felt like she was ruining my last hour of our vacation, like she was dropping something heavy into a moment that was supposed to be light. I asked her if she was scared, she said she was. I was too; the thought of anything happening to her punched the air right out of my lungs. I also felt this guilt that I couldn't rush off to be with her because I was extremely pregnant and didn't plan on being far from home after this trip.

I got off the phone with her and collapsed into Jeff's arms and told him the news. I said I wanted to be there for her first radiation treatment. He held me in this warm, loving way and reassured me that my mom would be fine.

It was another moment life backed me into surrender. I didn't want it, didn't choose it, but there I was, letting go because holding on wasn't an option anymore.

Shit, who knew this book was going to be so depressing? I swear, it gets lighter soon. But these months were so fucking heavy. February and March 2023 were no joke for our family.

We got home, and a couple of weeks later I packed my bags to go for my mom's first radiation treatment. She was so brave. It was the first of thirty treatments and it got much worse. Wear sunscreen, people.

I went back home after a few days in Winnipeg, where my mom lived, and was ready to nest. I was winding down at work because my SI joint pain was so bad the only way I was comfortable was to keep moving, because sitting, lying down, and standing were all so painful. Jeff, Frankie, I, and the dogs were living with Jeff's mom, Sandra, at the time as we sold our two-bed townhome and were waiting for our bigger home to be ready in April. Goldie was due April 30th, and our home was finished April 4, so we thought we'd be set up by the time the baby came.

Just as I was catching my breath, life shifted again. There's a point where you stop trying to predict what's coming and just start bracing for whatever arrives next.

When we went to bed on March 9th, I noticed baby was a little less active and made a comment to Jeff, but I could still feel some kicks, so I wasn't overly worried. I woke up Friday morning, my last day of work, a virtual baby shower planned for me in the afternoon. I was pretty excited to be off for seven weeks before baby came and just relax. I was stressed between moving, my mom's cancer diagnosis and treatment I wanted some time to get my nervous system in order.

I noticed the baby still wasn't active. I knew what we needed to do. I told Jeff and my mother-in-law that I was worried and lay down to count kicks and didn't feel anything. I called our midwife and she said to go to the hospital. Everyone thought I was being paranoid as that's exactly what happened with Frankie our first born. What was the likelihood that it would happen again? "Pretty fucking unlikely," I thought and still, my body knew. We packed our bags and headed to the hospital. I told my manager I may not make the baby shower.

We got to the hospital, and they rushed us in for monitoring. They heard Goldie's heartbeat right away. They told me to relax. They said they'd monitor for twenty minutes. Quickly after being connected, her heart rate was fast and getting faster. It was clear she was in distress. The alarm kept beeping and they said the baby probably needed to come out soon and started prepping me for what was next. I was thirty-three weeks pregnant having a normal pregnancy. How could this be happening again?

Jeff has serious anxiety and panicked soon after. I still felt calm, scared, but calm because I knew the baby would be okay. I always knew. They gave me a steroid shot in my butt and magnesium sulphate through the IV, which was honestly more painful than the emergency C-section that happened next. My entire body was burning; it felt like my skin was on fire, and I was sweating like the hottest fever and was certain I was going to vomit. I was thrashing around; my skin was crawling. My husband said it sounded like withdrawal, something he went through a decade or so earlier. It was horrible. Within ninety minutes of walking in the hospital, Goldie was out of my body.

What happened in the operating room is a blur. I was hopped up on meds, and Jeff was full of anxiety, but we had a playlist and put on Otis Redding for her birth because we were sure it was a boy and wanted to name him Otis.

Goldie's first surprise for us was that she came out as a girl. The doctor said she was perfect. They gave her a little bit of oxygen, but she looked good for a thirty-three-weeker. It wasn't until shortly after that things took a turn.

They took her away with Jeff as they sewed me up and wheeled me to recovery. I barely saw her, but I had a few pictures on my phone I could look at in recovery where I was immediately told to start collecting that liquid gold, colostrum that immediately drips out of your nipples. I collected these drops of honey, flipping through my phone of the three pictures I had of Goldie. I wanted updates. All the updates. I couldn't leave the recovery room. They kept coming in and rubbing ice on my legs to ask when I could feel it. It felt like eternity.

Jeff came back and checked on me, but it was a long walk from where I was to Goldie's room in the NICU. We waited to officially name her until I could meet her. By the time I was cleared to be wheeled over to her room, she had a feeding tube. Breathing rapidly but she was okay. She was so cute and tiny, and exactly like I pictured her, but a girl.

The first night was brutal. I was fresh out of an emergency C-section, stuck in a room across the hospital from my baby. Jeff slept beside me, and I kept asking him to go check on her — over and over, like a compulsion I couldn't quiet. My heart lived in my stomach all night. I barely slept, caught between pain, trying to pump milk, and the terror of knowing our tiny girl was all alone her first day earthside.

By the next morning, she was intubated, had multiple seizures through the night, and was being rushed for an MRI on her brain. We had gone to bed thinking she just needed some time to get stronger. What followed was a blur. For the next twenty days, until we were transferred to BC Women's Hospital, everything felt foggy. Close calls. Emergencies. Walking into her room to find ten doctors already there, surrounding my daughter. Her room was the room to watch. High risk. After several assessments and consults with neurology, genetics, and respirology, it was determined the best thing was for Goldie to be transferred.

The BC Women's/Children's Hospital was an hour drive without traffic from our home, but we knew it would be best for Goldie. It's one of the top children's hospitals in the world.

We settled into life at BC Women's Hospital.

We knew it would take time for Goldie to come home. We just had no idea how much time. Seven weeks would be plenty of time for her to be stable enough we thought...

Somewhere in that stretch of days, something shifted in me. I couldn't take life in weeks or months anymore. I couldn't even take it in days. My mind didn't have the capacity. I started living in tiny increments — the length of a pump cycle, the stretch of time between rounds, the fifteen minutes it took to walk downstairs and grab a coffee and come back to the room.

That's where the 15-Minute Rewrite was born, long before it had a name.

It started as a survival trick. A way to stay human when my life felt like a collapsing building. When everything was too big... too sharp... too heavy... fifteen minutes was the only amount of time my nervous system could tolerate. I couldn't plan a day. I couldn't map out a future. But I could survive a quarter of an hour.

That was the shift.

Not "I'll fix my life."

Just "I'll hang on for fifteen minutes and see what happens."

I didn't know what else to do, so I wrote.

At first, I used it to write when writing felt impossible. No pressure to be profound. Some days I barely made it five minutes. But I kept coming back, and every time I did, I proved to myself that I could show up without breaking.

Our brains trust small things, and once something feels safe, we stop resisting it. That's where momentum begins. Not with inspiration, but with safety. Some days I wrote past the time I'd given myself. Other days, I closed the notebook the moment the time was up and didn't feel like a failure. Either way, I kept my promise to myself. That one small promise opened a quieter kind of healing in me, the kind that doesn't announce itself. The kind that rebuilds you from the inside out.

Some days it felt like different versions of me were taking turns — the scared one, the furious one, the one just trying to stay upright. I'd sit with each of them for fifteen minutes. No more. It gave them space to speak without swallowing me. My body started to learn that feeling something deeply didn't have to mean drowning in it.

I didn't need an hour. I didn't need clarity. I didn't need a plan. I just need fifteen minutes. And fifteen minutes was enough to begin again.

Standing in those hallways, watching Goldie fight for every breath, I knew my life would never go back to what it was. There was a before and an after, and I was standing in the middle of them. Most of us don't start rewriting our lives because we feel inspired. We start because the ground gives out. This might be your moment, not because you wanted it, but because it came. What you do next is the first rewrite. If there's one thing those early days taught me, it's this: the body hears you long before the mind catches up.

Close your eyes. Feel what rises. Notice the truth underneath it.

Put your hand on your heart and say, "I love you. I am here."

Say it three times, gently.

Let your body hear you.

# F*CK WHAT THEY SAY

"Your intuition is guiding
you towards the truth.
Don't ignore it."

— MEL ROBBINS

AT SOME POINT, YOU HEAR SOMETHING THAT YOU SIMPLY refuse to take on as truth, not out of denial, but out of something deeper: a knowing that belongs only to you. Sometimes that knowing takes a minute, and the shame or guilt can swallow you whole first.

You are not becoming someone new. You are remembering who you've always been. The part of you buried under expectations, expert opinions, and inherited beliefs. Rewrite starts here: with your truth. The kind of truth that doesn't make sense on paper but rings louder than any algorithm or authority.

Everyone wants certainty. Your body wants truth. And something in you is done pretending those are the same thing. You're here because you're ready to trust yourself again. Life handed me a crash course in trusting myself: a meeting that would gut me to the core, the moment where knowing and fear collided.

### I DIDN'T UNDERSTAND ANY OF THIS YET. I WAS ABOUT TO LEARN IT THE HARDEST WAY.

In April, after being at the NICU for a couple weeks, they called a family meeting to discuss what the plan would be moving forward. There were about seven doctors and specialists in the room with Jeff and me. They told us there would be no new information discussed; it was more of a planning session to talk about next steps for Goldie. We were equal parts nervous and hopeful.

My stomach started to flip-flop as we sat down in the room and the neurologist, our first time meeting her, took centre stage in the conversation and pointed out the spots in Goldie's brain on the MRI. The room felt too bright for what was happening. Fluorescent lights, a huge boardroom table, and hard plastic chairs that squeaked when people shifted. I could feel Jeff's hand holding mine, grounding me, but my chest was tight. Her tone was clinical, clipped, like she was delivering weather updates instead of talking about our daughter.

The first time she said, "If she survives," something in my body snapped to attention. The second time, my ears started ringing. By the third, it felt like the floor dropped out from under me. I wasn't listening to her words anymore; I was watching her mouth move, trying not to throw up. Every sentence carved another inch off the future I thought we had.

"If she survives, she'll likely be immobile."

"If she survives, she'll be non-verbal."

"If she survives..."

She mentioned we'd be referred to Canuck Place within the first fifteen minutes of the meeting. Canuck Place is a children's hospice and respite centre. In that moment, all I heard was end-of-life. Later, they became our lifeline for the first two years of Goldie's life. But then, hearing Canuck Place and "if she survives" in the same sentence felt devastating. We're talking about our three-week-old preemie full of hope and possibility. She had a lot of questions about Jeff and my medical history, which I feel like we'd spent 100 hours talking about by that point. But when she asked me about miscarriages, I told her I had five pregnancy losses between Frankie and Goldie.

Her response: "Five pregnancy losses. Did you think maybe your body was trying to tell you something?"

I couldn't breathe for a second. This comment to a mother three weeks postpartum, positioning the blame for my daughter's state, went right through me. I'd had creeping thoughts of blame come into my mind in those first few weeks, thinking if we went to the hospital earlier, if I was less stressed from our move, etc. But Jeff quickly shut them down and reassured me.

We left that meeting shell-shocked, hollow, barely speaking. I wept. I didn't recognize it then, but this is where my intuition began fighting to be heard. A counsellor and the pediatrician came in to check on us afterward. They agreed Goldie's future was uncertain but reminded me I wasn't to blame. It didn't matter. The damage was already done. Her words replayed on a loop as I stared at my tiny, fragile daughter, the breathing tube taped to her face. I felt like I was drowning in grief, trapped beneath a tide I couldn't escape. What she said didn't stay in that room. It followed me home, crawled into my thoughts, and made itself believable.

I did this. That's what my mind kept whispering.

She's in pain because of me. It's my fault. My fault. My fault.

The loop wouldn't stop. The room felt grey, airless. I was furious at the neurologist for saying what she did, but even more furious at myself for believing it. It was one of the worst days of my life knowing that grim future for our tiny child fighting every day to be here.

I left the hospital a different woman than who walked in. We went to our new home that night, surrounded by boxes. We were still unpacking as we moved a day earlier. I was adamant I wanted to get back to the hospital, but I was exhausted, emotionally and physically drained. After all the talk of "if she survived" I didn't want to regret being away from her for one minute.

I told Jeff as I was packing my bags to drive back to the hospital, I couldn't get what the neurologist said out of my mind. I remember distinctly telling him I shouldn't be driving. I'm not feeling emotionally stable. He told me to stay, but I said I had to go. I couldn't be away from her.

It was dark outside, and I started driving, merging onto the freeway, turning left, and misjudging the distance of the oncoming traffic. I was T-boned at full speed. They didn't even honk. I never saw it coming. My little Prius was completely crumpled. The door couldn't open. I remember being worried about my C-section scar as I was a few weeks postpartum and the seatbelt pulled so hard against it and my boobs were so full of milk, they felt damaged from the seatbelt. I was in shock when the ambulance came.

I just kept saying, "I'm trying to get to the hospital to see my daughter. I need to get to the hospital."

I couldn't even call Jeff; I was in complete panic. The man whose car I hit called. That night, I didn't make it to see Goldie, but I was so lucky to walk away from the crash. I woke up the next morning and knew it hadn't been a dream. My body was sore. Shaken. Still trying to catch up to what had happened. Between the neurologist's words and the crash, it felt like everything had collapsed into one long night.

I wanted to be at the hospital with Goldie. I also knew I wasn't okay. I went to get a full assessment. The doctor said something that stayed with me. Because I didn't see the car coming, I didn't brace. My body didn't tense. It surrendered to the impact. That surrender is likely why I walked away with fewer injuries. Standing there later, sore and shaken, it hit me that I hadn't surrendered at all in the weeks leading up to that night. I had been bracing for everything. The doctors' words. The fear. The guilt. The what ifs.

My body knew how to soften before my mind did.

I was sleep deprived, dealing with postpartum, and living inside trauma. I didn't need more blame. I needed grace. That crash didn't just stop my car; it showed me what happens when I stop bracing against what I can't control.

I remember standing on the side of the road in the dark with my smashed car, my mind spinning, my body frozen. It felt like life was happening to me and I was just... gone. What shattered me most wasn't only the neurologist's words; it was how quickly my mind turned them into truth. Blame became the loop.

I've caught myself in that spiral more times than I can count. If it wasn't about the pregnancy losses, then it was Goldie's condition or my own health or anything else my mind could grab onto. When we're scared or stuck or desperate for answers, we look for someone to blame, and when there's no answer, blame becomes the substitute.

In the days after the accident, blame followed me everywhere. Into the shower. Into the car. Into the NICU. Even when no one said it out loud, my mind filled in the silence.

When you spend years outsourcing your sense of safety, value, and truth to others — family, religion, culture, institutions — doubting yourself becomes second nature. You learn that other people know better. You learn to hand over your clarity. Trauma doesn't just live in your memories. It starts narrating your life for you. And my narrator had only one line: *You did this.*

When that narrator gets loud, your intuition gets quiet.

For many women, especially high achievers, that conditioning goes deep. Being smart, agreeable, helpful, and "good" feels like the safest option. Being bold or emotional feels risky. Those stories never protected us; they kept us contained.

I came back to something I already knew but had never needed this deeply before. There isn't just one "me" trying to make sense of all this. There are parts inside us, each carrying their own fears, memories, and protective roles.

Trauma doesn't just create pain. It activates parts of us that learned how to survive long before we had language for what was happening.

There's part of you that wants to speak up. Another part that is terrified of being judged. Another that's exhausted trying to hold everything together. Another wants to burn it all down. The work isn't to silence any of them. It's to let the truest one lead.

Parts Work helped me understand how I could feel terrified and certain in the same breath. The voices inside you aren't random. They harden into limiting beliefs that shape every decision you make until you finally question them, and here is the question that matters: *What if those beliefs are lying to you?*

Limiting beliefs don't arrive loudly. They creep in quietly and start sounding like common sense. They tell you you're "just being realistic." But they aren't neutral. They shape your choices long before you notice they're speaking for you.

Beliefs shape what you think you deserve; intuition reminds you what's true. Intuition cuts through that noise, but only if you let yourself hear it. For me, those beliefs showed up in the hospital. I deferred to every doctor, even when something in my body knew differently. I used to say, "I'm not a medical expert." But I was a Goldie expert. Over time, I learned how to sound like both.

I had to override some deeply ingrained beliefs that I didn't know enough that I wasn't allowed to challenge the system, that someone else must always know better. But my intuition got louder. Trusting it saved Goldie from interventions she didn't need.

Your limiting beliefs don't need to be extreme to hold you back.

They can be quiet doubts like:

"I'm not ready to launch."
"Who am I to make that much money?"
"I'll probably fail anyway, so why try?"

They hide under goals, productivity, and comparison.

Often, they're just your subconscious trying to keep you safe. But what if safety isn't the goal anymore? What if expansion is?

When I left my corporate job, the limiting beliefs came rushing in: Will I make enough? Who am I without that title? Can I build something on my own? Some of those beliefs still whisper. New ones always appear as you level up, but that's the work catching them, questioning them, and choosing again. Your life is not meant to be lived in a box built by fear. Possibility is your birthright, and it begins when you decide to trust what you know even if no one else understands it yet. But beliefs aren't the only filter. The lens you choose in the middle of chaos will change the whole picture.

When Goldie was born, we were standing inside a storm of unknowns. The grief was real. The fear was real. The uncertainty was overwhelming. Yet, I knew I had a choice: I could collapse into it, or I could anchor into something else.

For me, choosing love, joy, and hope in the little things wasn't just a mindset; it was survival. That became my lens. Not because it erased the hard, but because it let me move through the hard without drowning in it. It didn't replace the fear; it just gave me somewhere steadier to stand. Even with that lens, the truth was still heavy.

The truth? That lens will shift sometimes. Your rose-coloured glasses will fog up. Grief and anger will change the filter.

From the moment Goldie entered the world, there was so much joy and so much pain. So much uncertainty, almost too much to bear. There were more apologies when

Goldie was born than congratulations. Most of the humans in our world come from a good place and we didn't need any apologies. There was so much to celebrate. Each day Goldie hit a milestone defying all odds felt like a miracle.

We all have baggage, and sometimes it felt like a dark cloud followed me around with sympathy and empathy about Goldie. It felt hard to carry and hard to talk about. For a while, I loved going places where no one knew me, so I didn't have to talk about it. Today is a new day. I wear my story, my trauma, my grief proudly as it's transformed who I am.

There was a deep pain, though, so much grief for what we thought our life, our babies, our families' life would look like and what it actually looked like. Finding the purpose in it all took a while. We (my husband and I) went through all the stages of grief, anger, fear, sadness. Great sadness.

I experienced the most selfless act I would never have expected from myself. When Goldie was finally home six months after she was born, she was in so much pain. Screaming, crying, drowning in her own secretions. I held her and whispered to her spirit that it was okay to go. It was okay to let go. If it was too hard to be in her body and to be on this earth, it was okay to let go. I'm crying all over my computer eighteen months after that moment because the amount of heartbreak I felt whispering those words to my baby was unbearable, but watching her suffer, thinking she may be staying for us, was also unbearable.

She chose to stay here with us, in her body. Her difficult and amazing body, to be Goldie, to change the world, to expand the hearts of hundreds of thousands. She chose to stay. The great pain I felt in these early months and still come back every close call, every ambulance ride, every hard conversation we have with specialists. That's when I learned what Rumi meant when he said,

**"THE WOUND IS THE PLACE WHERE THE LIGHT ENTERS YOU."**

Letting the light in didn't make life easier, but it made it clearer. That intuition isn't always loud. Sometimes it speaks in whispers you hope you never have to say out loud.

You can let the light enter you. Let it spread throughout your body and spread across the earth, much like Star in *Wish.* The feeling of light and warmth and safety if you let it in, that my dear one, is love, its purpose. It's everything. Goldie has been a catalyst for change since the day she entered Earthside. Following her has clarified everything that matters to me.

To put my oxygen mask on first, embody that light, and advocate fiercely for my girls.

To help busy women who are carrying guilt and shame the way I once did.

To support families living inside uncertainty, searching for hope and another way.

To choose love repeatedly, because when you do, something changes.

The more I chose love over fear, the more I felt something shift inside me. This wasn't magic; it was my brain rebuilding itself one choice at a time. Your brain is wired to adapt. To heal. To find the light again if you train it to.

That's neuroplasticity. Your brain rebuilds itself through the choices you make. So, when someone's opinion starts pulling you sideways, that's your cue to close the vault tight.

The vault is locked in. Not because life got easier, but because I did the work. My dear friend Heather Boersma once described it in a way that stayed with me. Your peace, your joy, your love, your knowing lives in a vault. Once it's in there, no one else gets a key. Not their doubt. Not their judgment. Not their fear disguised as concern.

The vault is where your power lives. You choose what goes in and you choose what stays out. Unfuckwithable. That's the energy.

A few months ago, my family was attacked online — strangers tearing into us, calling us horrible parents for sharing our story. The timing couldn't have been worse. Frankie was already struggling at school, and the weight of it all hit hard. I was gutted for about an hour, but the old story didn't get to run the show anymore. Then I remembered my truth. It lived inside the vault. I knew who I was. I knew the parent I was, and nothing a bully on the internet said, especially someone who didn't know me, my children, or our life, could take that from me.

What are you ready to put in your vault? You don't need a system for this yet.

Just honesty.

What belief, comment, or story about yourself are you ready to stop carrying? Write it down. Cross it out. Replace it with what is true for you. Say it out loud. Let your body hear you. This is where self-trust stops being theoretical and starts becoming real.

# THE REWRITE

---

*Part II*

# ANCHOR
# IN

"Clarity precedes success."

— ROBIN SHARMA

LEARNING TO TRUST TAKES TIME. LEARNING TO LOOSEN your grip takes longer. It's a practice.

I used to think manifestation was about getting what you wanted if you thought about it hard enough. But when Goldie was born, I learned it's so much deeper than that. I spent hours driving back and forth to the hospital, filling my mind with every manifestation book, podcast, and tool I could find. All I wanted to do was manifest Goldie's healing. I even messaged Katrin Zenkina of Manifestation Babe asking how to manifest for someone else. She told me something that broke my heart at first...

You can't manifest for someone else, but you can manifest the support you need. So, I started focusing on that, and the wildest thing happened. That same week, a stranger reached out. She'd survived a traumatic brain injury and felt called to share her story with us.

She didn't know us, but she believed in Goldie; she believed in us as parents. Somehow, that belief steadied me in a way nothing else had. People call Goldie fragile, but she's the strongest human I've ever met. If a 3.5 lb. baby in the NICU can fight for her future, I knew I could too.

Here's what I didn't understand yet: Sometimes trust doesn't show up as clarity; it shows up as people.

Not long after we started holding the vision, faith itself began to appear, not as a neat answer, but as people who believed in Goldie when her charts could not.

The unknown was massive. It still is.

Then they showed up, these healers, intuitives, energy workers, each of them arriving with this all-knowing presence. They didn't need a diagnosis to believe in her.

Or in me. They gave me something science couldn't: hope with no conditions attached. That belief, the idea, that any door could open, that anything was possible, kept me going through the darkest nights. It reminded me that not all answers live in charts or scans. While some of those relationships may have faded, the faith they helped spark stayed with me.

But faith can't just live in ideas or other people's beliefs; it has to take root in your own body. For me, that's where the rituals began.

There was a morning in the NICU when everything felt like too much. The machines were loud. The air was dry. I couldn't fix anything. So, I did the only thing I could: I started creating rituals to hold myself. Not because I was enlightened, but because I had no other choice. I only played 528 hertz, the frequency of love in the hospital. I would put my left hand on the back of Goldie's neck where her brain stem is and right hand on her stomach. It was how I reminded myself she was still mine, not just a body everyone else was managing.

Later, I heard something Andrea Crowder said on the *More Alive* podcast: If the earth split in two and your child was on the other side, you wouldn't question how. You'd build a bridge.

That's faith.

That's vision.

That's trust embodied.

Trusting the unseen is one thing. Living it beside a 3.5-pound baby fighting for her life is another.

The rituals I created were more than survival. They

were the only things that gave my nervous system enough footing to stay present with Goldie when everything in me wanted to collapse.

Every morning in the NICU, I anchored myself in three things: the energy I was bringing into the room, the love I could offer, and the grip I was willing to loosen. Staying rooted in my own energy so I didn't drown in the fear around us. Choosing love, even when the day felt brutal. Letting go of the outcome, because control was a luxury I didn't have.

I wrote. It was the only way to quiet the noise in my head. The Five-Minute Journal became such an important practice to keep me sane. When I flip through those pages now, the things I listed as gratitude still undo me: Goldie coughed. Goldie came off her high-flow oxygen. Snuggling. Tiny things. Miracle things.

One of the things I used to write in my five-minute journal was "snuggling." But snuggling didn't mean what it sounds like now. In the NICU, it took two nurses to place Goldie into my arms. She was intubated. Covered in wires. Machines breathing for her. Monitoring her heart, her oxygen, her brain. During one phase, she was part of a brain study. More than twenty tiny leads were attached to her head, each one feeding data into a monitor beside us. Once she was in my arms, I couldn't move. Not an inch. If I shifted wrong, alarms would sound. Tubes could dislodge. Everything felt fragile.

I felt guilty asking to hold her and desperate not to let go. I wasn't surviving by accident. I was being held together by practice.

# THE PRACTICES THAT HELD ME TOGETHER

**528 Hz:** the frequency of love. It kept the room soft when nothing else was soft.
**Presence:** savouring the moments because we didn't know how many we would get and we still don't.
**Acceptance:** letting myself unravel without shame.
**The MVP:** one minimum-viable priority, because survival required simplicity.
**Coffee:** arguably the most sacred of all hospital rituals.

These rituals kept me steady so Goldie could feel safety through me. Just enough so I could stay soft without falling apart. They became my blueprint for every hard season that followed.

## WHAT YOU'LL LEARN IN THE PAGES AHEAD

This isn't a book about Goldie. It's a book written *because* of her. Through everything she's taught me about the nervous system, resilience, miracles, and rewriting your life even when it feels like it's burning to the ground.

You don't need a diagnosis or a breakdown to begin again. You just need one moment of truth. One decision that changes how you move forward.

Goldie gave me mine. Now I'm passing it on to you.

# THE 15-MINUTE REWRITE

**I CREATED THE 15-MINUTE REWRITE™ OUT OF DESPERA-
tion.** It was born in a hospital room during the darkest, most uncertain months of my life.

Goldie had just entered the world with a rare, medically complex condition no one could name. Every day was a barrage of decisions and diagnoses. I was in survival mode, mentally, physically, and emotionally. Somehow, I still had to show up for my baby, for my family, and for myself, if there was anything left.

What steadied me were the moments I permitted myself to come back to myself. They were never longer than fifteen minutes.

A slow walk around the hospital.

A cry in the shower.

A lukewarm coffee and a journal entry that began with: "I don't know how to do this."

That was it. Just a few minutes of truth and breath in the chaos.

That survival season gave birth to something sacred. A rhythm. A ritual. A way back to myself in fifteen-minute windows.

## WHAT IS THE 15-MINUTE REWRITE™?

It's a trauma-aware, nervous-system-safe way to transform fifteen minutes at a time. It's not a productivity hack. It's a pause that belongs to you, in a world that constantly pulls you outward. It's 1% of your day.

It's a presence practice. A return inward. A gentle listening.

What if fifteen minutes was enough? Enough to feel something again. Enough to hear your own voice beneath the noise. Enough to start coming back to yourself, gently, powerfully, without burning your life down.

## CHOOSE YOUR REWRITE

This isn't a routine. It's a relationship with yourself, with your nervous system and with what matters most. Ask yourself:

"What would fill my cup right now?"

"What could I do in the next fifteen minutes to honour my truth?"

Some days that answer will be breathwork. Some days it'll be a nap. Some days it'll be staring out the window and quietly noticing.

Here are some ideas to start with. You'll find your own as you follow the practice:

Slow walk
A good cry
Tea in silence
Voice notes to your future self
Breathwork
Pull a card
Stare at the sky
Journal

If you're someone who likes a little structure, here's a gentle framework you can learn:

REGULATE: Calm your body (breathwork, tapping, body shakeout)
REFLECT: Connect to truth (ask: "What do I need right now?")
RECLAIM: Take one aligned micro-action (a small move that feels true)

This is how I began to rewrite my life. Not all at once. Not with a plan. But moment by moment, fifteen minutes at a time.

So no, it's not always pretty, but it's powerful because this is the real work. We think the "work" is the big moment. The leap. The transformation. But the work is in moments like this. Quiet. Internal. Humbling. Full of self-confrontation and tenderness. One brave move at a time.

**Why It Works**
It meets you where you are, not where you "should" be
It helps your nervous system learn that small changes can be safe
It respects your bandwidth
It builds radical trust through consistent micro-action
It dissolves the pressure to do it all perfectly

You don't need a whole new life. You just need a moment of truth and then another and another. That's the magic.

You'll notice that the 15-Minute Rewrite looks different throughout this book. That's intentional. Some days you need grounding. Some days clarity. Some days permission. Later in the book, you'll find a *Rewrite Map* that lets you choose a practice based on what your nervous system needs in the moment. You don't have to do them in order. You don't have to do them all.

Start with the one that feels possible.

## IT'S NOT ABOUT THE TIME

Fifteen minutes is arbitrary, but it's attainable. *It's the space between disappearing and choosing yourself. It's the moment where you decide: "I get to take up space in my own day."* Once you remember how to take up space, you start building a life that actually supports you. That means fifteen-minute rituals. Boundaries that hold. Support systems that exist in real life, not just on your vision board.

This is where you shift from reacting to choosing. From proving to protecting your peace. From surviving the week... to finally designing it.

I knew where I was blocked on my calendar and my book. It was the evenings. I was so exhausted by the time we put the kids down, I wanted to zone out and watch some stressful escapism shows with my husband Jeff. Stay up later than I should and wake up too tired. It felt like all I had energy for, but it was just a habit. I had a strong morning routine that changed my life, and it was time to get myself on track with an evening one.

So, I did, and not all at once. Right now, I'm giving myself fifteen minutes to work on my book after the kids go to sleep, and guess what? It's been an hour and I'm still writing. The story I was telling myself that I was too tired to do anything but zone out was true and writing gave me energy and lit me up in a way binging a show on Netflix didn't.

Where in your twenty-four hours are you stuck? Where can you make space for fifteen minutes to rebuild? Put it on your calendar as a daily reminder now. Once you've cleared a little space, don't rush to fill it with pressure or productivity. Fill it with something that helps your body exhale.

One song and a slow sway.
Steam rising from your tea.
Five steady breaths on the back step.
Anything small that registers as safe.

Joy doesn't need to be grand to be powerful; it just needs to be felt.

Start there. Keep it simple. Repeat often.

Throughout this book, you'll see 15-Minute Rewrite™ invitations at the end of key chapters. These are quick, accessible practices to help you embody the rewrite in real time. These aren't tasks. They're tools designed to meet you exactly where you are. Some will ask you to move. Others to reflect. Others to reclaim a part of yourself you've been ignoring.

Take what you need. Leave what you don't. But whatever

you do, keep coming home to yourself one small moment
at a time.

# OWN
# YOUR
# ENERGY

"Your energy is your
greatest currency."

— JORDAN HOECHLIN

 unseen bandwidth your life depends on. When you learn to honour it, protect it, and pour purposefully from it, something extraordinary happens. You begin to sense what strengthens you and what steals from you, and that's where this story begins.

## THE MAGPIE AND THE NEST

In a place not quite forest, not quite sky, a nest holds. Not fragile, not flimsy. It's woven from story threads and saltwater, lined with lioness fur and mother's bone. This is no ordinary nest; it's survival turned sacred, grief turned gold.

Here lives the Queen. Not of palaces, but of rebuilding. Of fire that warms. She doesn't posture. She protects. And still, the magpies come. They always do. Drawn to the shimmer, they circle. They say they care, but they stare. They pluck feathers, not to help but to have. They carry grief-glitter back to their hollow nests.

For a time, she let them. Softened. Explained. Justified. Until she remembered she is the nest. She is the gate-keeper. Not for show. Not for consumption.

You are the nest.

Magpies will circle your life, too, disguised as concern. Curiosity dressed up as care. They don't come to nourish; they come to extract. And here's the truth I learned too late: they only get in if you let them.

So, build your nest with discernment. Reinforce it with light. Protect the baby birds, your creations, your healing, your legacy.

You don't owe your grief to anyone. You don't owe your energy to curiosity disguised as care. Ask yourself: Is this gaze nourishing or extracting? Is this presence safe?

Magpies will always exist. But you? You are the nest. You decide who gets in. What I didn't understand yet was how literal this would become once Goldie came home.

Catastrophe, tragedy can attract all sorts. Most people come to support, and some come to stare at a building burning down or a fatal car accident. Some people don't come to help. They come to watch. And that kind of attention costs more energy than silence ever did. Be mindful of those plucking feathers from your back, seeming like they want to help, but are slowly taking your energy. Asking all the questions, wanting updates; you don't own anyone anything.

It's not just metaphorical. Protecting your energy isn't only about who you let close emotionally; it's also about how you protect what's most sacred in the physical world. When Goldie finally came home, she was about six months old. Taking her out into the world for the first time terrified me. We needed so much equipment: tubes, monitors, suction, and her little helmet drew even more attention.

Everywhere we went, there were stares. Curious eyes. Sometimes pity.

People want to get close to babies, the same way they do to pregnant women, as if boundaries don't apply. Once, a woman reached into her stroller to touch her belly, not realizing she had a feeding tube. After that, I made a tiny sign that hung from her stroller: I'm sensitive. Please keep your distance. It was for her safety, of course, but sometimes I wished we all had a sign like that, a gentle reminder that we, too, are sensitive. That we need space, softness, permission to exist without intrusion.

People often asked, "What's wrong with her?" and I hated that question, the way it reduced her to diagnosis and difference. Most people meant well; they just didn't have the language. I'd smile and answer the only truth that ever mattered:

"Nothing. She's perfect."

But protecting your energy isn't just about strangers in public. It's about the invisible load you carry every day — the one no one else can see.

The thing about energy is it's invisible, but you feel every ounce of it. Whether it's a magpie at your door or a tension in your chest, your body knows. Before you can rewrite your life, you have to reclaim the energy it takes to live it. Capacity isn't time. It's your nervous system. It's the invisible bandwidth that lets you hold what life throws without collapsing.

Once you know your capacity, you start to see where your power has been leaking and where it's been roaring the whole time. If "in the fire" cracked you open and helped you trust yourself again, this is about building the container strong enough to hold it all. You can't rewrite your story from survival mode. You can't reclaim your voice if your system is fried. You can't stand in your power while your boundaries are being hijacked.

Protecting your energy isn't selfish. It's sacred and it's where your life starts to feel like it belongs to you again. Once you begin protecting your energy, something else happens: You start remembering who the hell you are. Not just a person trying to survive the week, but someone with fire. With presence. With boundaries. With don't-fuck-with-me energy.

Ready is just a decision. Ready to live, ready to love. Ready to jump. This is your life. You get one shot. You get to decide the energy you bring into the room. You get to decide what you stand for. What feels like a hell yes in your body. What feels like a fuck no. That's your power. Own it.

Once you recognize that power, you start to see it everywhere, especially in the places you least expect it. Even in a hospital room. Even in a tiny body fighting for life with more clarity than most adults ever find.

You can be full of love, open-hearted, and still fiercely boundaried.

What is don't-fuck-with-me energy? It's exactly how it sounds.

Early on in the NICU, Baby Goldie embodied this energy and got louder and fiercer as she got older. She also taught me how to do the same. She'd let her care team know what's up. By the time we left the NICU after six months, the walls in her room were plastered with rules the nurses and my husband and I wrote down. Don't swaddle her, she likes cuddles, bum taps, don't this, do that. For a 3.5 lb. baby, she owned her power. She knew what she wanted; she still does. We can learn a lot from babies. They are so simply focused on survival, sleep, food, love, and poop. That kind of clarity comes before we're taught to override it.

With Goldie, it was harder to know her likes and dislikes at the beginning apart from the obvious, pain, intubation, bright lights etc. Now, she yells at you when you turn off her favourite movie, *Sing.*

I think the magic thing about babies is they come born with that don't-fuck-with-me energy early on. The ones who want to be held constantly, or eat constantly, whatever they want, they want it now. They are ready and let the world know with fierce screaming, crying, and tantrums.

For Goldie, that energy wasn't just theatrics or a cute quirk; it showed up in the most literal, high-stakes ways. It shaped how we made decisions in the NICU, how we vowed to protect her, and how we measured every hospital visit afterward.

It was also her way of communicating what she needed when she couldn't use words. That's what led to one of the most powerful lessons we learned in the NICU: every person, even a 3.5-pound baby, needs a roadmap.

Something we learned early on at the hospital was that Goldie couldn't communicate in the typical ways, so her care team built her a system. Her preferences, her triggers, her positioning needs, all of it went up on the wall. Instructions about how to hold her, how to angle her bed, and what to do when she desatted. Eventually, her nurses created a whole algorithm, a step-by-step protocol to keep her stable.

When we brought her home, that roadmap came with us in a binder. That binder has evolved into something deeper, not just care instructions, but a way to understand her, to advocate for her, and to honour who she is. This was the moment I understood that energy protection is not just a feeling, it's a system.

Holding that binder made something click: Goldie had a system. The rest of us are out here moving through adulthood without ever writing down what helps us feel safe. We don't write down what we need when we're overwhelmed. We don't tell people how to love us when we're flailing. We don't even ask ourselves: What helps me feel safe? What calms me down when I'm in the spiral?

But maybe we should. Maybe that's what this book is, a kind of roadmap. Not a manual, but a personal system. Like Goldie's hospital walls, full of reminders, cues, and loving truths to come back to. And just like her bed needed to be tilted at an unusual angle to help with drainage, maybe your healing needs something a little different, because what works for others might not work for you.

This is about knowing what you need.

The more clearly we understood what Goldie needed, the more fiercely we protected it, especially in the moments that asked the most of us. Goldie didn't want to be intubated — a breathing tube placed down her throat, and her tiny body made that very clear. In her first four weeks, she was intubated and extubated several times, a cycle that's risky for any newborn and can cause permanent airway damage. Goldie fought it. We made a promise when we left the NICU that we would never intubate her again.

Nearly two years later, and we still haven't broken that promise. We came close a few times. Most recently, Goldie had a surgery to put ear tubes in to help with her hearing and Botox in her salivatory glands to help with her secretions, and they said it was more than likely she would have to be intubated for the procedure. The procedure I wasn't worried about, but the intubation and sedation had me stressed for weeks.

Jeff and I both didn't want to break our promise to our girl, especially knowing the risks of intubation. They said they had the operating room booked for four hours.

After all that fear, we couldn't sit in that waiting room another second. We both needed to move our bodies and get the energy out. We walked. We walked and we walked. We walked to this beautiful park and saw so many amazing groups of seniors doing Tai chi, dance chi, and fan chi. It was perfect as we climbed the small hill of Queen Elizabeth Park in Vancouver to look at the view and wander through the gardens to see more than six different groups of people practicing Tai chi.

A hummingbird flew above us as we wandered through the garden. Another energetic force, and I knew Goldie would be fine and was reminded that our energy is our currency and it was all around us. I'd been holding it together in the pre-op room. Now the tears came as we walked, climbed and watched these beautiful humans gracefully move their bodies in the early morning sun. I felt the nervous energy subside.

I trusted in my inner knowing that Goldie would be fine before we got the call. Knowing this walk was exactly what we needed. In this case, it was very much a "don't fuck with Goldie" energy I was embodying. We carry that a lot; I don't know if we learned it from Goldie or she learned it from us. Either way, it's always there. When you have to advocate hard every damn day for yourself (if you're a Goldie) or for your child, that don't-fuck-with-me energy is right under your skin like an invisible mask or superhero costume ready to be turned on/put on at any moment. Ruffle a feather, deny a service, say something isn't possible and watch it come out in full vengeance. It's the grit that makes things possible. That pushes things forward.

When they came out of the operating room two hours later, we received a call from the doctor saying she did well. She was breathing on her own, didn't require a breathing tube, and we were so relieved. I truly feel this was a testament to her strength and her don't-fuck-with-me energy.

Goldie is a force and she knew what she didn't want, and her body made it work so she didn't need it. Her body had spoken with absolute clarity, and in a way, ours needed to catch up.

When your life requires you to fight for the small mercies, protecting your energy stops being optional and becomes holy work. We carried that vow into every hallway of the hospital, into every decision, and even into the dark places where the mind tries to sort the hurt.

One morning, I woke from a dream where I'd finally said every hard thing to a close family member. When I woke up, I was back in the truth of it: this is about energy.

Your energy is the most sacred life force you have. When you're around people carrying fear or toxicity, it seeps in. You can visualize bubbles or cut cords or cleanse your space after, but if someone is in your home, in your field, in your family, that energy lands. It lingers.

With Goldie, this became crystal clear.

We've had nurses and doctors come into our lives with energy that either expanded our hope or crushed it. Some treat her like the miracle she is and others still treat her like she's fragile, not fully human, like the most important thing is wiping her face, not seeing her heart. That kind of energy doesn't belong here, because here's what I know: when you surround yourself with people who believe in miracles, who radiate that energy, you rise. Your whole world rises.

But when you stay around energy that diminishes you or your people, especially your children, you dim. Your nervous system starts to believe what they say. Your heart starts to close. And your light? It flickers.

I've become fiercely protective of our home, our field, our peace, especially for Goldie, because she is all power. She is light. Anyone who can't see that, anyone who chooses not to see that, isn't welcome in her world. Not anymore. Her energy needs protecting, and so does mine.

But protecting your energy isn't just about people, it's about patterns. It's not just what you say no to externally, but what you unconsciously say yes to internally. What you consume consumes you.

Once I started noticing the energy of the people around us, I began noticing something else — the energy I was unconsciously giving away in quieter, subtler ways.

Here's what I've learned while recovering: what you consume matters. Not just food but content. Energy. Inputs. I noticed how often I reached for comfort when what I actually needed was nourishment. Binging shows. Eating cookies in bed. Staying up too late. As a result, I've been waking up feeling hungover. Foggy. Sluggish. Like my nervous system is trying to recover while I'm sabotaging it with sugar and noise.

I even started dreaming about some of these shows because they were the last thing I saw before sleep. Of course, they followed me. But I felt like garbage. If I'd spent that time with breathwork, or journaling, or visualizing the life I'm building... I would wake up with that energy in my body instead.

I had to learn the difference between comfort and nourishment.

Comfort consumption isn't bad. Sometimes it's exactly what our inner child needs. But true nourishment, the kind that supports healing, is different. It's quieter, more intentional. This wasn't just a lesson in healing. It was a lesson in input. Now I know better. I began paying attention to what drained me, what filled me up.

Once I saw the pattern, I couldn't unsee it. I stopped

tracking my to-do list and started tracking my capacity. Not just what was on my calendar, but how it made me feel in my body. This is how the Energy Audit was born, and it became one of the core practices in The 15-Minute Rewrite™.

Now it's your turn to reclaim what you're carrying.

# YOUR 15-MINUTE REWRITE

**The Energy Audit**

REGULATE — Calm your body (breathwork, tapping, body shakeout)

REFLECT — Connect to truth (use the prompts below)

RECLAIM — Anchor in aligned action (take one micro-move below)

**Regulate:** Take a breath. Settle into your body. Reflect on the past forty-eight hours (or longer if you'd like).

Where did your energy feel most alive?
Where did you feel most depleted?

**Reflect:** Use the two columns on the next page to track your patterns.

DRAINS ME: Things that pull you away from yourself. (e.g., Scrolling late at night)
FILLS ME UP: The things that restore or expand you. (e.g., A solo walk, voice memoing a friend)

| DRAINS ME | FILLS ME UP |
| --- | --- |
|  |  |

Now, choose one or two things from each list:

What are you committed to prioritizing this week?

What are you ready to offload, cancel, or shift?

**Reclaim:** Your Energy: Intention Setting

I release _____________________ and reclaim my

energy for ___________________________.

I release _____________________ and reclaim my

energy for ___________________________.

I release _____________________ and reclaim my

energy for ___________________________.

What's one small, specific way you'll honour your energy this week?

Write it down. Make it real. Let this be your return to centre.

# NAVIGATE PLOT TWISTS

"If you change the way you
look at things, the things
you look at change."

— **WAYNE DYER**

PLOT TWISTS DON'T JUST CHANGE YOUR PLANS; THEY change your identity. That's where this story begins.

Life is full of plot twists, isn't it? Learning to meet them with grace is its own skill. Letting go of how you thought things would go is another. When it comes to pregnancy, pregnancy losses, and the big life moments, those twists can carry real grief, devastation, and anger.

We used to joke about "getting better writers." I didn't realize then how literal that idea would become or how little control we'd actually have over the story that followed. I often feel that when we're in uncharted territory again, it's a test from the universe for the next level up. We were sitting in a family meeting room at Canuck Place, the children's hospice in Vancouver. It was quiet, dim. Soft cozy chairs. Nobody was drinking the tea. Or the fresh-baked cookies, what they are known for. The kind of space that's been carefully designed to hold grief.

Goldie had been in and out of the hospital four times that winter. Her body was so fragile. Every time we brought her in, it felt like the interventions did more harm than good. We were living in constant emergency mode. At home, she was calmer. More regulated. Less poked and prodded. But we were drowning in uncertainty.

The team gathered us for the meeting, the head nurse, a palliative care doctor, a counsellor and asked us the impossible question: What is best for Goldie? We already knew the answer. Jeff and I had talked about it the night before, both of us wrecked by the truth we didn't want to say out loud. It was time to change her goals of care.

That meant no more hospital runs. No more aggressive

interventions. A pink 'Do Not Resuscitate' form in the nurse's binder. The plan was to keep her home, keep her warm, keep her held and keep her comfortable. They prepared us gently, but directly:

**"YOU MIGHT WAKE UP IN THE MORNING AND FIND HER NOT BREATHING."**

I'll never forget the stillness in that room. How the walls felt like they were holding their breath with us. Part of me felt like we were giving up. The deeper part of me knew we were choosing her. We were choosing love. We were choosing to parent her the way she needed most.

Goldie spent the next eight months under comfort care. Eight months of not knowing what would happen next. Then something miraculous happened. She started to thrive.

Grief had trained us to brace for the worst, so when her body chose a different path, we almost didn't trust it at first. But miracles don't erase the unknown; they just teach you how to hold it differently.

Eventually, we were able to lift the DNR. We rewrote her goals of care again. That pink DNR sheet came out of her binder and into the shredder. Lifting a form doesn't erase the fear that lived under it. She kept showing us what was possible, not just with her body, but with our hearts. Even now, the reality is that this level of care might be needed again.

There were parts of the story I found myself avoiding. Old wounds that still sting. But this is what surrender looks like. This is what letting go means. And this is what love does: it chooses presence over perfection. It chooses snuggles over certainty. It says stay, even when everything feels like it is falling apart. Once you have stood in that kind of truth, everything else rearranges itself.

This is Goldie's magic. Her fragility and that conversation shifted how we approached everyday life. It reminded us to make our own magic in every moment we were given.

The rest started to fall away. The noise, the pressure, the things that do not matter. What stayed was the clarity, the softness, the pure love between a parent and a child, and that extra tug that comes with the uncertainty of having a sick one. You breathe their skin a little deeper. You hold them a little tighter, and you notice the magic that has always been there. Because when you're making the most of every moment, magic shows up everywhere, even in the rawness. Especially there. Sometimes, it's as small as a tiny joy, one bright ordinary moment that gets you through the darkest days.

But not every plot twist looks like hospice meetings and pink DNR forms. Some are quieter but relentless, middle-of-the-night 911 calls, weeks of hospital stays, and anniversaries spent in plastic chairs. Those moments require a different kind of grace, the kind you build in the daily details.

Jeff and I, over the last two years, have gotten good at navigating emergency situations with Goldie. She has been to the hospital eight times since she was discharged from the NICU in 2023. All emergencies. All the middle-of-the-night trauma bay entrance. Fifteen doctors rushing in to stabilize her. This is her level of fragility, where one cold or flu that Frankie brings home from school becomes life-threatening for sweet Goldie.

We had learned how to survive the big plot twists at home. What surprised me was how the smaller ones still found ways to test our capacity. After months of hospitals, alarms, and vigilance, we'd taken a much-needed family trip to Hawaii. A brief pocket of rest. Sun, water, time together. A chance to let our nervous systems settle while Goldie was in the safe respite care of Canuck Place.

We were still in the air when the call came. Goldie had a fever. Tested positive for COVID and had to be discharged early, with nowhere to go. My worst fear, happening in real time.

Then the second hit: her emergency contact tested positive too. With COVID circulating, we couldn't bring our home nurses back either. The safety net we rely on every day disappeared in a single phone call.

Years ago, this is the kind of moment that would have sent me straight into survival mode. The spiralling, the catastrophizing, the frantic planning ten steps ahead. I used to live there. But this time, something different happened. I felt the fear. I felt the ground shift. Then I began to soften. Goldie was stable. Her only symptom was a fever, and I knew her body. I knew her cues. I knew her tells.

We also realized something that landed with both weight and pride: we were the best caregivers she had in that moment. Other than her nurses, no one in the world knows her as we do. That truth used to terrify me. Now it anchors me.

I looked at Jeff. I looked at Frankie and I realized I'm not the woman who used to live in hypervigilance. I felt my rhythm kick in, the one I've been rebuilding for years. The practices that steady me without needing a checklist. The instincts I trust now. It was enough to keep me grounded in the moment instead of abandoning it. And because of that rhythm, we did not panic.

We didn't reroute the whole trip out of fear. We stayed. We rested. We let the sun work on our nervous systems. Most of all, we let it be true that Goldie was okay. It hit me later, by the water, watching Frankie play in the waves: the old version of me would have flown home immediately. Not out of logic, but out of fear.

This version knew we were safe enough.
This version trusted our capacity.
This version did not abandon the moment we came here for.

That is the miracle of a rewritten nervous system. Plot twists stop being the thing that breaks you. They become the thing that shows you how far you have come. After living through plot twists that take you to the edge, you start to see them differently. Not as punishments, but as invitations.

Maybe that's the whole point. Life isn't supposed to be perfect. It's supposed to be an adventure. What if the reframe is this: even the hard parts are just wild detours in the story? Starting a business. Changing careers. Becoming a mother. These shifts feel so high stakes, so heavy. But what if they're just part of the quest?

When you travel, you expect delays. You miss a train.

You end up in the mountains of India without a sweater (true story) and what do you do? You buy a sweater. You adapt. You reroute. You keep going.

I used to put so much pressure on myself: Make the sales. Build the program. Hit the goal. Everything felt high stakes, heavy, loaded with meaning. But what if it's just an adventure? What if it's meant to be messy, funny, surprising — and that's the point?

What if you let it be easy? What if you let it be fun? When you take the pressure off, the magic shows up. And the next sweater? You'll know exactly where to find it. If you can make magic in a hospital room, you can make magic anywhere.

If you've lived through enough plot twists, you start to realize grace isn't passive. It's a frequency. How you move, what you believe, the energy you hold — it all sends a signal. That's the part you can control, even when everything else feels uncontrollable.

Once you understand energy that way, everything shifts. You always get another chance to choose the signal you're broadcasting. You don't have to force it or fake it. You just begin again.

So, let's practice. Let's change the frequency right here, in the smallest way, and choose again.

## YOUR 15-MINUTE REWRITE: HOLDING GRACE IN THE CHAOS

Set a timer for fifteen minutes.

**Regulate:** Close your eyes and put one hand on your heart, one hand on your belly.

Take slow breaths and remind your body: *I'm safe in this moment.*

**Reflect:** Journal on this question: What unexpected plot twist am I navigating right now (big or small)? What emotions does it stir up in me?

Let yourself be honest.
Messy.
Unfiltered.

**Reclaim:** Write down: *Even in this plot twist, I choose to...* Fill it in with one truth, action, or value you want to hold onto.

Examples:
I choose to keep humour alive.
I choose to rest.
I choose to believe there's another way.

That's how you hold grace in the chaos.
Not by fixing the plot, but by choosing who you are inside it.

# CLEAR THE SHIT THAT'S BLOCKING YOU

"You are not finding your answers, you are finding your courage."

— BRIANNA WIEST, *THE PIVOT YEAR*

PRESSURE WILL ALWAYS REVEAL THE THING YOU DON'T want to look at. I was avoiding more than I wanted to admit. I'd been holding everything, my family, my business, my book, the endless medical complexity of our life, in a full-body pressure cooker. Just when I thought I had a grip on it, the little fucker returned.

The old story. The voice that whispers *you're failing before you've even begun.* She was familiar: failure-to-launch me. The girl who once believed staying small was safer than being seen. My mentor asked why I was so angry she'd shown up again.

"What if you just welcomed her?" she asked. "Let her come in. Let her sit beside you. What if you said... welcome back. I love you."

It disarmed me. Goldie has been my greatest teacher, but even now, I catch myself pushing her edges, wanting her body to do things it simply can't do yet. Then comes the guilt, the crash, the remembering: she is miraculous exactly as she is. Why was I so unwilling to give myself the same grace?

My book felt like a mess. I was trying to force clarity, hold every loose thread at once, control the story like it was a problem to be solved instead of a truth to be lived. It was allowed to be messy. Maybe the identity I kept trying to outrun wasn't failure. Maybe it was part of the launch.

This wasn't just about parenting or writing. It was about who I became when fear took the wheel. Underneath all of it was one question: who am I without my fear? Free. Unfuckwithable.

Fear rarely walks in announcing itself. It slips in quietly, disguised as logic, planning, responsibility. It convinces you that staying small is wise. It convinces you that you're safer gripping tight than expanding. Every time I named it, the grip loosened. Every time I integrated the scared part instead of silencing her, I built trust with myself.

## EVERY BLOCK IS A DOORWAY. EVERY PATTERN IS A PORTAL.

After years of learning to "manage" my life, I started to notice the subtler ways fear dressed itself up as responsibility, humility, even love. It's a shapeshifter. It tells you you're just being realistic while quietly keeping you small. I saw it most clearly in my marriage. Jeff and I are both wired to over function, me with emotion, him with action. When Goldie came along, we built our survival around efficiency: suction machines, alarms, med schedules, tag-teaming night shifts. One day, I caught myself measuring our marriage by productivity instead of intimacy. I realized fear had disguised itself as control.

Control isn't safety; it's scarcity wearing armour. Fear is clever. It will hide under self-sacrifice, perfectionism, planning, even spirituality. It will tell you that waiting for the "right time" is wise when it's actually avoidance. The mind will offer a reason to delay: the inbox, the laundry, the better version of you that hasn't quite arrived. But those reasons are costumes for fear.

Here's how I started naming mine.

# THE ROOTS OF SELF-SABOTAGE

Self-sabotage isn't weakness. It's protection that's outlived its purpose.

1.   **Unworthiness:** "I don't deserve this. Who am I to even try?"
→ Keeps you from showing up, asking, launching, or receiving.

2.   **Fear of Abandonment:** "If I change or succeed, will they still love me?"
→ Shows up when you associate growth with loss.

3.   **Unprocessed Grief:** "It doesn't feel fair to feel good right now."
→ Can cause you to unconsciously mute joy or ease.

4.   **Visibility Trauma:** "Being seen got me hurt before."
→ Keeps you small, quiet, or hiding behind other people's brands.

5.   **Chaos Addiction:** "Peace feels... weird."
→ Recreating drama to avoid stillness that feels unsafe.

These fears don't vanish with awareness, but once they're named, they lose authority. They become something you can work with instead of running from. Jeff helped me see that in real time. He once told me, "You plan like you're preparing for disaster." He wasn't wrong. I used to treat every possibility like a fire drill. My nervous system didn't know the difference between danger and daily life.

I started testing a new response: curiosity instead of control. When my mind spiraled, I asked, *What if nothing's wrong?* It felt unsafe at first. That's how I knew it mattered.

I learned this first in my body. Movement rewires fear faster than thinking ever will.

Fear will always whisper reasons to stay put. Your job is to move anyway, through trembling knees, wobbly voice, shaky breath. Movement is how you teach your nervous system that safety and expansion can coexist. When resistance shows up, I start looking for what it was protecting.

The moment you bring the fear into the light; it starts to dissolve. You don't have to banish fear. You only have to stop mistaking it for truth. Every loop has an exit if you're brave enough to stop running in circles.

Integration always begins with awareness. You can't rewrite what you won't look at. I used to think healing meant fixing. If I just found the right tool or teacher, I could finally silence the chaos, but wholeness isn't about muting the noise; it's about learning to listen differently. For years, I tried to out-think my feelings. My brain ran board meetings on anxiety while my body waited patiently for permission to exhale. The mind was loud; the body was loyal. When I finally slowed down long enough to hear her, she whispered the truth: presence, not pressure. That's what I mean by awareness: it isn't analysis, it's intimacy.

Not something to fix, but something to lead with awareness. Whenever I pushed through exhaustion, a younger part of me, twelve, maybe thirteen, was still trying to earn love by performing. Awareness meant noticing her before she hijacked my day. Sometimes I'd literally say, "You can rest now."

Those tiny acknowledgments became my rewiring. Goldie taught me the same lesson through her work with Anat Baniel Method (ABM). ABM isn't about force or repetition; it's about re-patterning the brain through gentle, intentional movement. The practitioner doesn't push the body to comply; they invite it to awaken. I watched it happen again and again. One quiet shift in her body, a tilt of the head, a micro-movement in her spine would reorganize everything. The room would feel electric. Presence over pressure.

ABM showed me that transformation isn't achieved; it's allowed. Progress comes from attunement, not aggression. In one of the strangest, most tender turns of this journey, hope came to me through a voice note. She was a mother I'd never met in person, the cousin of my energy healer, who lived across the country. Living on a ranch. Living a life that, by all medical logic, was not supposed to exist.

Her daughter had been born with a severe brain injury. They told her she wouldn't survive more than a few weeks. If she did, they said, she would never thrive. They prepared her for loss, not life. Her daughter is six now. She is alive because her parents refused to accept that there was only one way forward.

They took a different path, Chinese medicine. Acupuncture. ABM. Somatic therapies. Horses. Nature. Regulation. Devotion. Trial and error. Relentless love. Not instead of medicine, but alongside it. Not recklessly, but deliberately. The doctors were stunned, not because miracles don't happen, but because devotion changes what's possible.

This mother and I spent hours sending voice notes back and forth. Long ones. Messy ones. Late-night ones. She told me about the moments she almost broke. The treatments that didn't work. The ones that slowly did. The fear. The grief. The hope she learned to protect instead of explaining. She didn't promise me outcomes. She didn't sell certainty. She just showed me what was possible when you refuse to abandon your child or yourself.

Listening to her changed something in me. There was another way. Someone was already walking it, and if she could do this, maybe we could too. I still dream of taking Goldie to that ranch one day. Of watching her body soften around the horses. Of letting her nervous system learn safety in the presence of something steady and alive. But even before that happens, the miracle has already arrived. It arrived in the knowing that there's always another way. That devotion matters. That intuition is not foolish. That sometimes the thing that saves you doesn't come from a protocol, but from another woman saying, "I found a way and I'll walk it with you."

Believing another way is possible didn't start in my mind; it started in my body. If your nervous system doesn't feel safe, it won't let the new story stick. That's why awareness has to reach the body first. When fear patterns loop, it's your body trying to protect you. It remembers old danger and confuses it with the present. The work isn't to erase the pattern; it's to teach your system a new ending.

Neuroplasticity is real. Every time you respond differently, you lay new tracks. Every breath of awareness is a new connection forming. That's the rewrite: turning old fear into new familiarity.

## BELIEF SYSTEMS AND THE SAFETY OF YOUR SUBCONSCIOUS

Your subconscious mind runs the show more than you realize. It isn't background noise, it's the driver behind your choices, resistance, and patterns. Anything new feels unsafe to your subconscious. Your system craves safety, not success, but the moment you rewire even one belief, one story about who you are or what's possible, your subconscious starts to open new pathways. Your nervous system learns to regulate around the unfamiliar. That's where the magic happens.

As Dr. Joe Dispenza says, "Nerve cells that fire together wire together." Your brain doesn't know truth from repetition. It only knows what you return to. Awareness is the moment you stop returning to the old story.

The human brain isn't fixed; it's living, responsive, rewiring all the time, which means the voice that says you're too old, too late, not enough? That's not the truth, it's training, and anything trained can be retrained.

When you combine mindset, self-awareness, and

compassionate self-leadership, you don't just change your thoughts, you change your identity. You shift how you see yourself and what you believe is possible.

When I couldn't find my way out of a loop, I came back to two truths: what is this protecting, and what would feel safer and truer right now. Whether your loop is fear, age, or an old inherited narrative, the practice is the same:

Name it. Disarm it. Choose again.

# YOUR 15-MINUTE REWRITE: THE BLOCK BREAKER

**Regulate:** Breathe. Shake it out. Move your body.

Let yourself settle just enough to tell the truth without flinching.

**Reflect:** Write down the loop that's been running your day, or your decade. The one that keeps pulling you back into the same reaction, the same hesitation, the same stuck feeling.

Let the scared part of you speak without shame.
Ask her: *What do you need to feel safe enough to try?*
Don't argue with the answer. Just write it.

**Reclaim:** Finish this sentence, exactly as it wants to be written:

It's been feeling like _______________________________.

And even with that, I choose to believe _______________.

Say it out loud. Let your body hear it.


You don't have to fix everything.
You don't have to bulldoze your fear.
This part isn't here to sabotage you.
It's here to protect something that matters.


The next time you feel your shoulders tighten and breath shallow, pause. Put a hand on your chest and ask: *What part of me is trying to keep me safe right now?*


Listen before you lead.


Respond instead of override.


That's how blocks soften.
That's how protection loosens its grip.
That's how the rewrite begins.

# GO
# INWARD

"Knowing yourself is the beginning of all wisdom."

— ARISTOTLE

I THOUGHT GOING INWARD WOULD FEEL PEACEFUL, BUT it dragged up everything I'd been avoiding. Going inward isn't about discipline. It's about devotion.

Commitment says, *I'll try if I have time.*

Devotion says, *I'll matter enough to make time.*

Devotion is the quiet vow to keep showing up for yourself even when no one's watching, even when the progress is invisible.

When you practice devotion, the work stops being another thing on your to-do list and starts becoming the way you come home to yourself.

Devotion doesn't always look like peace. Sometimes it looks like ugly crying on a country road and choosing yourself anyway.

It had been less than twenty-four hours into my long-awaited solo retreat. I was supposed to be writing, but instead of feeling triumphant, I was crumbling. My phone rang. The principal from my older daughter's (Frankie) school. She had run out of class again. She's five and in kindergarten. The school wanted to talk. Frankie got on the phone, her voice tiny and trembling.

"I miss you, Mommy."

Guilt hit me like a freight train. What kind of mother leaves? What kind of mother chooses solitude, creativity, herself? Was this even worth it?

I wiped the tears from my face and stepped back onto the gravel path toward the little cottage where I was staying, but I didn't make it far. Something stopped me. A cluster of baby chicks, fluffy, warm, sleeping in a little pile nestled under heat lamps, surrounded by soft straw and two quiet, watchful ducks.

I broke, right there, in the middle of this hobby farm off a side road. I cried for Frankie. I cried for Goldie. I cried for myself. I didn't realize how much I was carrying until I stopped moving. Those chicks reminded me of the NICU. Of the days when my daughters were tiny and covered in wires and tape and tubes. When we couldn't hold Goldie, only offer "hand hugs" through the incubator window. When snuggles weren't even allowed.

### "SAFE IN THEIR SNUGGLE PILE."

That's all I ever wanted for my babies, to scoop them up and hide them under my own hands. But motherhood isn't always a soft nest. Sometimes it's a storm, and sometimes, we're the ones who have to leave the pile to rebuild ourselves.

I stood there crying, remembering the weight of that early trauma, how quickly guilt can morph into shame. How grief hides in moments you don't expect, but also how symbolic healing can sneak up on you, in a farmyard, with some chicks, after a phone call.

I didn't go home. I stayed at the cottage. Forty-eight hours to write, to breathe, to remember myself. That's what I needed. The truth was, Frankie was fine. I was staying ten minutes from my house, and I'd be home by bedtime. It was a reminder of how fast motherhood can flood the system and how quickly guilt tries to convince you you're doing it wrong. What made it unbearable wasn't the moment; it was the accumulation.

The weight of all the moments stacked on top of each other until my body felt like a permanent emergency room. We live in the cracks of a system built for the cookie-cutter life. Goldie doesn't fit. Frankie doesn't fit. Our family doesn't fit, and when you don't fit, you fall, and fall again.

Without a diagnosis, we're constantly advocating just to receive the bare minimum. Explaining how complex Goldie is. Proving how high needs she is. Translating our reality into language that the system might take seriously.

Frankie has celiac disease, and with it, a deep fear of food. She's been exposed enough times to know exactly what happens next. Ten to twenty rounds of vomiting. Days of brain fog. A stomach that won't settle. A body that can't focus. Still, it's brushed off because it won't kill her. A busy server doesn't see the aftermath of a mistake. They don't see the days that follow. We do.

Frankie is considered the most high-needs child in her kindergarten class. The school is trying, they really are. We've been encouraged to pursue assessments, to untangle trauma from anxiety from neurodivergence. We've been working with a child psychologist ever since Goldie's birth.

Frankie has woken up to an almost empty house more times than a five-year-old ever should, seven times to be exact. Ambulance already gone. Emergency team in motion. Grandma waiting quietly in the kitchen.

Somewhere between the paperwork, the pleas for funding, and the meetings with politicians, I lost track of myself. We've been on the news. We've rallied. We've demanded better nursing support. We've fought for funding, and still, it takes a toll.

On days that feel impossible, I've spiraled. I've ugly cried. I've wanted to give up. But as a parent, there's no giving up. In this one wild, precious life, you don't give up. But you can pause, you can ask yourself: What is my MVP today, my Minimum Viable Plan? What's the absolute least I need to do to get through? Eat cookies for breakfast. Drink too much coffee. Take a nap instead of answering emails.

Today, I joked that journaling wasn't enough. "I need a whiskey," I said, and it was only 10:30 a.m. Alcohol used to be my coping mechanism for years. On both sides of our family, generation after generation, alcohol was the tool to numb. Jeff and I were both determined to break that cycle. On days like today, when the pull to numb is strong, I find another way. My whole chest tightens first, that's always the tell.

As a family who lives in the crack, who has to make noise to make progress, I can't be numb. I have to be alive, not numb, not always in fight mode (sometimes advocacy feels like that). Today, I choose softness, going inward. I used to think what I needed was commitment, another plan, another promise to keep. But what I was craving was devotion. Commitment says I'll do it if I can. Devotion says, I'll do it because it's who I am. Devotion is the bridge between self-awareness and self-love, loyalty that doesn't depend on motivation.

Even on the hardest days, I carry her, the version of me who chased freedom like oxygen. She still lives inside me, somewhere beneath the appointments and emergency calls and gluten-free snacks in my purse. The wild girl who booked flights, crossed borders, and believed anything was possible.

Before motherhood, freedom was everything to me. I chased it across cities, countries, continents, believing that movement itself was meaning. After high school, I backpacked through Australia with my best friend Danielle. We were wild and fearless; we even ran away once, forging letters from our parents to cross the border and covering seven states in five days. I know, as a mother, I'll be karmically repaid for that one.

After university, I left again. I found a remote job and lived coast to coast in Canada, then drifted through California, Mexico, and Amsterdam. New places lit me up — they still do. When I met my husband in Vancouver in 2016, it was another kind of adventure. We fell in love fast, married within six months, and built a life that matched our pace. First dog. First house. First daughter. Then another dog, another house, and finally Goldie.

The version of freedom I knew was gone. It took me years to understand that the greatest adventure of all isn't out there. It's inward. Somewhere along the way, freedom stopped meaning movement and started meaning escape. I wasn't chasing cities anymore; I was trying to outrun what I didn't yet know how to sit with.

Yes, travel still calls to me, but most of us will spend more time exploring new cities than exploring ourselves. If I had spent even a fraction of the energy I spent chasing cities on actually listening to myself, who knows what I might've found sooner.

It took me a longer than I'd like to admit. I invite you to look at your vacation time, your travel budget, your escape fantasies and ask: What if I flipped this inward? (Not instead of, but in addition to.) Because the inward adventure turns out to be the most transformational of all. The bravest thing I could do wasn't to leave; it was to stay. To go inward, to feel everything. To keep writing, even when it hurts.

### WHAT DOES IT MEAN TO GO INWARD?

It means getting radically honest with yourself.

It means pausing long enough to hear what's true, beneath the noise, the pressure, the stories.

It means turning toward your life instead of running from it.

Going inward doesn't mean fixing everything. It means feeling what you've been avoiding and staying long enough to hear the truth.

Going inward isn't just a concept; it's a practice you return to when running stops working. That's the inward path, a return to yourself, one breath at a time. When you go inward, you don't always find answers. You find honesty. You find capacity. You find yourself. And from there, everything else becomes possible.

# YOUR 15-MINUTE REWRITE: THE INWARD ADVENTURE

**Regulate:** Close your eyes. Feel your feet on the ground. Notice the weight of your body where it's supported.

Whisper to yourself:
*I am here.*
*I am safe to turn inward.*

Let your breath deepen just enough to stay.

**Reflect:** Ask yourself, honestly:

*Where have I been chasing relief, certainty, or validation outside myself?*

*What have I been avoiding feeling, knowing, or naming within?*

Don't rush to make it sound wise. Write what's real. If resistance shows up, include that too. That counts.

**Reclaim:** Finish this sentence in writing: *Going inward for me right now would look like...*

Then choose **one small way** to invest in your inner life this week.

Time.
Energy.
Money.
Boundaries.

Not as self-improvement, as self-respect. Going inward isn't retreat; it's return.

# GET RUTHLESS ABOUT WHAT YOU REALLY WANT

"Attention is the rarest and purest form of generosity."

— SIMONE WEIL

FOR YEARS, I DIDN'T KNOW WHAT I WANTED, ONLY WHAT I thought I should want.

Guilt tells you to shrink.

Culture tells you to settle.

Fear tells you to wait.

But desire? Desire is a compass. It doesn't explain itself. It points.

And if you listen long enough, it will lead you straight to the life that's asking to be built. No one's going to roll out a red carpet for you. If you want the dream, you have to build it from your joy, your purpose, your fire. Not from working harder or proving yourself, but from a ruthless kind of clarity. A certainty that says: *this is mine.*

## HERE'S THE PARADOX: YOU NEED BOTH THE GRIT AND THE GRACE.

The ruthlessness to show up and the softness to release control over how and when it happens. Yin and yang. Push and surrender. That's how I rewrote my story, by doing things scared, by refusing to outsource my clarity, and by choosing, again and again, to go after what I wanted, even when it made no sense to anyone else.

You can't do it alone. Getting clear doesn't mean carrying it all by yourself. That's where the village comes in. It takes a village to raise any child, but parenting Goldie takes more than that. My mom used to threaten to burn my skateboard when I was a teenager, terrified I'd hurt myself. Sometimes I think about that, how even with all her love, she couldn't protect me from the life we live now. Parenting Goldie is extreme parenting. There's no sugar-coating it. Still, the lesson stuck: risk and resilience go hand in hand.

We also have a choice. We get to wake up and decide how we want to feel, what we want to pursue. That part's still ours, and that's why I've stopped chasing someone else's version of success.

I chose when to ask for help from the village. We all have that choice. I know we are incredibly fortunate to have such a strong community willing to step up and support us when we ask. It's hard to ask, but we do it. When Goldie was first born, a friend set up a GoFundMe for us, and we were reluctant. We kept saying we were fine. She kept saying, "Let the people help." She was right. The Go-FundMe has helped us keep our home, pay for unexpected medical bills and treatments as we were navigating the toughest months of our lives.

I will forever be grateful for our dear friend Sarah for pushing us to create the GoFundMe. I honestly don't think we would have survived the first year of Goldie's life without it. I am in tears thinking about it. Before I cry my eyes out at this cafe thinking about the generosity of friends, family, and literal strangers who have carried us, I'll say this: surrender isn't just about letting go. It's about letting in.

It's being okay asking for help and receiving it. Ditching the guilt of needing support. Releasing the shame of not being the strong one. What do you have to prove by going it alone, especially when it's impossible?

The real work isn't conquering anything. It's claiming what's already yours, and that brings us to the deeper practice: *receiving.* Asking is only half the equation. The shift happens when you let yourself take support being offered. When life feels like it's not going your way, this might be the part that is missing. You may be closed to receiving.

I kept pushing, proving, performing, bracing against the very support I prayed for. You can't receive what you don't feel safe to hold.

When Goldie was born and our GoFundMe was launched, I wanted to prove I was worthy of every dollar. I didn't know how to simply receive. I was hustling for help and missing the whole point. You can't rewrite your life if you're still resisting support.

Receiving is a nervous system practice. It's surrender, a softening. A radical declaration that you don't have to do it all alone anymore.

Let that land: you don't have to do it alone.

Receiving doesn't have to be abstract. You can practice it right now in small, practical ways. Ask yourself: Where in your life are you blocking support? What kind of help or love are you craving and have you actually asked for it?

**I am open.**
**I am ready.**
**I am willing to receive.**

You don't need a plane ticket or a new identity to find yourself. You need fifteen minutes and a willingness to be honest. This isn't about self-indulgence. It's about self-respect. But clarity inside your home or your heart isn't enough. At some point, you have to get loud. Ruthless vision demands a voice.

The thing about asking for help and being ruthless about what you want is you need to get loud about it. Not only in your own body, out in the world. We got loud and ruthless when it came to Goldie. Relentless in our quest for treatment, support, funding, all of it. We went to news outlets when our nurse funding was cut. We rallied the community of Goldie supporters when the funding was pulled and we were at the risk of losing our jobs, home, everything. The thing about getting ruthless and loud is you don't ever know who is listening. Our ruthlessness led to other families getting loud too and also getting the nursing funding and support they needed.

The roar gets people's attention, but it isn't the volume that keeps them listening. It's the clarity underneath it. The calm. The steadiness. The part of you that knows what you're asking for and doesn't disappear while you ask.

I didn't learn how to communicate by trying to sound confident or polished. I learned by needing something badly enough to stop cushioning my words. By speaking plainly. By staying in my body instead of apologizing for taking up space. There's a kind of authority that comes from that. Settled. Grounded. Earned.

When I know what I want, you can hear it in how I speak. There's less explaining. Less over-justifying. Fewer apologies baked into my sentences. Not because I've hardened, but because I'm no longer negotiating with myself first. Boundaries start to feel cleaner, too. Not sharp. Not defensive. Just clear. Protecting my time, energy, and capacity stops feeling selfish and starts feeling necessary, and the guilt that used to trail behind those decisions doesn't stick the way it used to.

There's a presence that comes with that kind of clarity. A way of being fully in the room instead of rehearsing what to say next. People feel it. They feel steadiness. They feel safety, not because I'm trying to hold everything together, but because I'm not split inside myself anymore. Wanting more stops feeling like something I need to explain away. Desire becomes directional instead of embarrassing. I can hold gratitude for what is without pretending I don't want what's next. Wanting doesn't make me greedy or ungrateful. It makes me alive.

This isn't about getting it right. It's about being willing to stand by myself.

Speaking up when something doesn't work.

Letting myself want what I want without shrinking it to fit someone else's comfort.

Releasing the reflex to make myself smaller so other people feel less threatened.

I've learned that the gap between wanting and receiving is almost always a story. When that story shows up, this is what I do.


## THE BELIEF BRIDGE EXAMPLE

I come back to this practice whenever the gap between what I want and what I'm living starts to feel heavy. Not dramatic. Just dense. The moment when desire is clear, but belief hasn't caught up yet. When I know what I want, but my body is still braced.

I don't start by trying to convince myself of anything. I start by telling the truth, the unfiltered one. The version that isn't trying to sound healed or optimistic. The sentence I'd only write if no one was watching. My nervous system doesn't respond to affirmations it doesn't trust.

This practice isn't about forcing a new belief. It's about building a bridge between what's true right now and what I'm willing to believe next. Here's what that looks like in real life.

## Health Rewrite

It's been feeling like my health and energy are an uphill battle. Like aging, bloating, and fatigue are just part of the deal now. Despite that, my body is responsive and resilient. When I slow down and listen, it meets me there. I feel lighter, clearer, and more energized than I have in years.

## Abundance Rewrite

It's been feeling like growing my business requires sacrifice. Like success must cost me my health, my presence, or my peace. Despite that, I build from alignment, not burnout. My work reaches the people it's meant to. Money supports my life instead of consuming it.

**Family Rewrite**

It's been feeling like time as a family slip through the cracks. Like we're managing instead of really living. Despite that, we are deeply connected. There is laughter here. Presence. Ordinary moments that once felt impossible.


That's the work. Not pretending things are better than they are. Not bypassing the hard parts. Just choosing a belief your body can hold.
Now you try.

# YOUR 15-MINUTE REWRITE: THE BELIEF BRIDGE

**Regulate:**
Close your eyes.
Put one hand on your chest. One on your belly.
Breathe until your body stops bracing for impact.

Say this quietly, even if part of you resists it:

*I am safe to want more.*
*Nothing bad happens if I tell the truth.*

If your body feels charged, move for ten seconds.
Shake. Stretch. Exhale hard.
Then stop.

**Reflect:**
Choose **one** area of your life that feels tight right now.
Not everything. The one you keep circling.

Health. Money. Work. Identity. Parenting. Your body.
Your future.

Write this sentence exactly as it comes out. Don't edit it:

*It's been feeling like* _______________________________.

Now answer this honestly:

*If this changed, I'm scared that* _______________________.

Then write the belief that's been running the show:

*The story I've been telling myself is* _______________________.

Don't make it spiritual.
Make it accurate.

Now write the belief you're willing to practice **today.**
Not forever. Just today:

*What might also be true is* _______________________________.

If it feels slightly uncomfortable, you're in the right place.

**Reclaim:**

Circle one sentence you just wrote.

Read it out loud. Let your body hear you.

Now ask:

*If I believed this sentence for the next twenty-four hours, what would I do differently today?*

Choose **one** action. Small. Specific. Unimpressive.

Send the message. Cancel the thing. Rest without apologizing. Ask the question you've been avoiding. Stop explaining yourself. Do that. Nothing else. You don't need certainty to move. You need honesty.

That's how the bridge is built: not with vision boards, but with truth, followed by action.

# HEAL WHAT YOU'VE BEEN AVOIDING

"Our bodies know the truth
long before our minds
are willing to listen."

— **CLARISSA PINKOLA ESTÉS**

I KNEW IT BEFORE THEY SAID THE WORDS OUT LOUD: SKIN cancer. One more thing I didn't have the capacity for. One more confrontation with mortality.

Even though it's the "best kind to get," the phrase doctors love to toss around, it still hit like a threat. Goldie had surgery that weekend. My nervous system was already maxed out. I was on stress leave, trying to stabilize, and then this. This is what I mean when I say our bodies know the truth long before our minds are willing to listen.

It shook me more than I expected. Just two years earlier, my mom had been diagnosed with a serious form of skin cancer. She needed daily radiation for six weeks. Her surgery was rough. We were scared and what made it worse was the guilt that surrounded all of it, my guilt, her guilt, the way we couldn't be there for each other the way we wanted to be.

I flew home to go to her first radiation appointment. Goldie was born a week later. I needed my mom more than I'd ever needed her, but she was in the middle of her own survival. Goldie was fragile. Every day felt uncertain. There was this haunting parallel: both of them, my baby and my mother, battling unknowns in their bodies. It stirred something ancient in me. The weight of the matriarch role. The fear of not being able to carry it all, because what happens when the one holding it all starts to fall apart?

I didn't see it coming. I thought I could keep holding everything together and then cancer shows up, and suddenly I'm doing the exact thing I tell women not to do, pushing down my own need and burning out all over again. The fragility of all of it. I'm learning again that self-care isn't a luxury. It's survival, especially when you're the matriarch.

The weight wasn't just emotional, it was cellular. Sometimes, that weight forces us to confront identity itself, the stories we hold about strength, wellness, and who we think we're supposed to be.

You think you know who you are until life hands you a plot twist, and not the "do it for the plot" kind. I'm talking about the real ones, the kind that make your chest tight at 3:30 in the morning as you crawl out of bed to whisper an eight-minute voice note into your phone in the dark bathroom.

I spiraled. I was working with my therapist, doing all the things, journaling, meditating, eating well, getting outside. Yet, I was struggling. My doctor suggested medication, an antidepressant to help with the anxiety. I couldn't accept it, not at first. My identity said I shouldn't need it. I'm strong. I'm high functioning. I have tools. I help other people.

Here's what I've learned about rewriting your life: Sometimes rewriting begins by letting go of who you think you're supposed to be. The shame I felt around needing help, then lying to my doctor about taking the pills, the inner dialogue that I was somehow failing, wasn't about the medication. It was about the story I was still holding about what it means to be "well." About what it means to be strong.

That was the moment I realized this wasn't just about fear. It was about healing. This cancer and this moment forced me to look at all of it: The guilt. The perfectionism. The pressure. A deep belief that I had to white-knuckle my way through pain to prove I was resilient. But what if resilience isn't about pushing through? What if it's about allowing support?

I see now that identity isn't static. I never wanted to identify as someone who had cancer. Even though it feels strange, like calling an angry mole a battle. But it was a battle. One more twist in a chapter that already had plenty. Identity evolves as we do, through motherhood, illness, and every plot twist that forces us to become someone new.

We don't always get to choose the plot twist, but we always get to choose who we become in response. If you're in the middle of your own spiral, holding a story or a diagnosis or a decision you never asked for, I want you to know this:

You are allowed to be scared.
You are allowed to accept help in whatever form
it takes.
You are allowed to pause, rest, process, heal when
you're ready.

You're still strong. Still worthy. Still capable of rewriting your story, even from the most broken chapters. That's what The Goldie Effect is truly about. Sometimes, healing doesn't begin with a plan or a breakthrough. Sometimes it starts with something quieter, the body whispering what the mind won't always slow down long enough to hear.

It took me eighteen weeks on short-term disability before I rested, and even then, it took a cancer scare to make me stop. That's how deep the programming runs. But I'm done going through the motions of "wellness." I'm done pretending my journey fits inside a formula.

Surrender doesn't guarantee outcomes, but it creates the margin healing needs. If you've ever wrestled with what it means to receive support, especially as a woman conditioned to be the strong one, let me tell you: you don't have to earn your rest. You don't need to justify your softness. You don't need to act resilient to be worthy of relief.

We moved into our new home three weeks after Goldie was born, and a few days after she was transferred to BC Children's Hospital. It felt brutal to be away from her, setting up a house we were supposed to have settled into months earlier. It was meant to be a season of nesting, not surviving. The day after we moved, I hung decals in her room, soft desert tones, tiny palm trees, a little wall made just for her. I wanted her to feel like she had a place in this new world.

But that's as far as I got.

Her room slowly filled with boxes, baby gifts, cards, and flowers. On nights I wasn't at the hospital, I'd sit in there alone, waiting for her to come home. It felt wrong to have a nursery without a baby. Months later, when we learned Goldie would need at-home nursing, we realized her room would never be what we originally imagined. It wasn't just her space anymore; it was also a nurse's room, a medical room, a place of constant care. The thought of a stranger in there every night was almost too much to bear. Frankie had slept beside us for six months as a newborn; Goldie never would.

Now, that same room is full again, not with waiting, but with life. The nurses who once felt like strangers are now family. There are eleven of them, and every single one loves Goldie fiercely. They've celebrated her milestones, cried with us through the hard nights, and saved her life more times than we can count.

We've been woken by alarms in the middle of the night, to nurses calmly calling out vitals or dialing 9-1-1. We've shared coffee on the stairs after long nights, holding both relief and gratitude. Our home is busy, loud, and alive, a constant rhythm of care, but this community of support, this chosen family, has turned what once felt heavy into something holy. That was the first time I understood that healing doesn't always look quiet.

Sometimes, healing is a house full of love and machines humming through the night. Letting go gave me space to finally listen, not to the noise of my thoughts, but to what my body had been trying to say all along.

If you've ever been the strong one, the caretaker, the overfunctioner, this part is for you. I've been talking for years about growth, resilience, transformation. How to rewrite your story. Regulate your nervous system. But it hit me recently, like tears-in-the-car, pull over on the side of the road kind of big: I've never actually talked about healing. Not the kind that lives in the body. Not the kind that makes you stop, makes you rest. Makes you feel what you've been trying to think your way around.

I talked about growth. Resilience. Pushing through. I talked about tools and practices and mindset shifts, but

I was still living from the neck up, treating my body like something to manage instead of something to listen to. It's wild, because once you see that, it's obvious.

All that time I spent trying to out-think the pain, push through the fear, keep showing up... I thought I was transforming. Maybe I was, a little, but I wasn't healing, not until I started moving. Not until I danced barefoot in a forest. Not until I stopped sitting in front of my computer trying to think my way out of a situation and started listening to my body instead.

It was breath. It was sweat. It was singing too loud and dancing like no one was watching and finally letting myself feel. That scared me more than any rewrite, because healing is messy. It's not a checklist. It's not a morning routine. It doesn't always look productive, and it doesn't come with a guaranteed outcome, but it's everything.

It's what we crave when our hearts feel broken, and we try to fix it with a new job or another strategy. That's when I finally understood — this was the work my body had been asking for all along. This is the piece: for me and for Goldie. For the parts of me I didn't even know were still carrying pain.

Healing didn't start when I tried harder. It started when I loosened my grip. One small moment at a time. You don't need a bigger breakdown or a longer leave of absence or the perfect retreat to begin. You just need one moment of truth. One breath. One quiet yes. To truly sit there in the discomfort of healing. Notice what you're feeling without trying to change it. Process it. Start there.

Let it be enough.

Awareness is only half the medicine. The other half is what you live next.

Letting go is what nearly broke me. Not the fear of dying, the fear of losing my edge. The woman who didn't hesitate or shrink or need permission to take up space.

I told myself I was taking a break, that I was focusing on healing, but secretly I was spiraling. I was afraid momentum was slipping away. Afraid my story was too heavy. I did what many of us do: I sabotaged. I numbed out. I hid behind logic and labels. Even with all the tools, the therapy, the awareness, I still found myself in the loop because I was scared.

You don't always have to push. Sometimes magnetism lives in the pause, in the moment you stop forcing and let your body come back online. Healing is the choice to reorganize the calls of the body, to slow down long enough to hear what it's been trying to tell you, and to answer with rest instead of resistance.

Remember the roadmap we made for Goldie, the binder, the wall of notes, her likes, her boundaries, her comfort cues. It wasn't a manual; it was a love letter. A survival plan. A declaration of what helped her thrive. What if you had one too? What helps you feel safe? What shuts you down? What opens your heart again?

Healing isn't about being perfect. It's about remembering what holds you, what brings you back. What gives you breath when you're about to break. That's your roadmap. Start writing it.

If you're wondering where to begin, start with this, a simple fifteen-minute way to listen, move, and begin again.

# YOUR 15-MINUTE REWRITE: LET THE BODY LEAD

**Regulate:**

Find a quiet place. Sit or stand however your body wants. Place one hand on your chest, one on your belly.

Breathe slower than usual. Deeper than usual.

Not to calm down. Not to fix anything.
Just to arrive.

Let your body know you're listening.

**Reflect:**

Ask yourself, gently: What part of me has been asking to heal, but I've been too busy, too afraid, or too focused on coping to hear?

Don't force an answer. Let a sensation, word, memory, or image rise.

This isn't about understanding. It's about noticing, without rushing it away.

**Reclaim:**

Put on one song. Let your body respond however it wants.
Sway. Stretch. Shake. Sit still.
Move slowly or wildly. There's no right way to do this.

When the song ends, write one sentence that honours
what came up.
Something simple. Something true.

*Example:* The part of me that carried everything can
rest now.

That's it. Fifteen minutes to step out of your head and back
into your body. A practice you can return to anytime the
noise gets loud or when you're finally ready to listen.

# MAKE YOUR OWN MAGIC

"I've been a thousand
different women."

—EMORY HALL IN "MADE OF RIVERS"

BECOMING ISN'T ALWAYS AN EXPANSION. SOMETIMES it's shedding old skin, like a snake, transforming into a new woman. I've grieved every single one of them.

I've ended up in an identity many times I didn't even recognize. Full of jealousy, distrust, scarcity. Somewhere on the journey of motherhood, I completely lost myself. I became worried all the time, the fun, wild, crazy adventurer, a woman who truly ran with wolves, was gone. I missed her. She was replaced with a manager, a mother, a martyr. My body ached for adventure; it missed her. She was buried alive under the responsibilities and fear of motherhood.

I never cared what anyone else thought until I became a mother. Was I doing it right? It was so fucking lonely knowing I didn't want to be my mother but had no idea who I was becoming instead. Being a new mom in 2020 was so tough. Add the isolation of becoming a mother on top of the isolation of a pandemic. I completely lost myself. I felt incredible guilt for bringing my child (Frankie) into this world of uncertainty. That same guilt came back when Goldie was born but for a different reason.

The guilt of her life's uncertainty, the pain she was in, how challenging it was to navigate her body. Honouring the version of me who didn't think Goldie was going to make it, the version of me who made the hardest choice to shift to comfort (palliative) care for Goldie before her first birthday, to the version of me whispered in her ear it was ok to say goodbye if her body was too painful to be in. I weep for those women. This book has been so healing but also reliving the trauma of those versions of me has been eye-opening. I didn't realize how many of them were still living inside me.



I've done a lot of work rewriting my identity, and I still am daily. Sometimes it's by choice, being reflective, spending time checking in on your life, how you feel when you wake up and what feels off. Sometimes, it's inspiring, sometimes it's excruciating.

When I was faced with the decision to leave my corporate job of eighteen years, I cried for days. It wasn't a choice. I wasn't functioning in my high-level role anymore, working three days a week juggling medical appointments, ordering supplies, nursing schedules, researching miracle treatments for Goldie. In retrospect, I was pretty checked out at work. Who could blame me? I didn't even realize how checked out and burnt out I was until my manager put me on a performance review improvement plan. I was in shock.

I've always been a high performer, and when she used the term "low performance," it was like she was talking about someone else. I was terrified, I was mad. My immediate reaction was defense, which I'm learning is always my reaction when I feel threatened in any way. It felt like my manager was threatening my entire family.

I spiraled hard, thinking we were going to lose the house. I couldn't stop weeping because I thought of how so many families like ours are faced with this situation, losing their jobs, their income, because of the complications of having a child like Goldie. Some families have no choice but to give up their child and put them in the foster system. I knew over my dead body this wouldn't happen, but I wept for all the families that had no choice, because the system is broken. Because a sweet angel like Goldie requires so much support the parents can't work to pay their bills to put food on the table.

I took a medical leave. My manager was just doing her job, but it was so gut-wrenching. I fell into a deep depression. I think this corporate identity I was holding on to for so long and everything I was doing to hold it all together, finally fell apart. This abrupt invitation to disrupt my life was exactly what I needed to gain the clarity, even though I couldn't see my way out yet.

All the questions swirling in my head of losing health insurance, a reliable income, but the part that was the hardest was the loss of my identity in corporate leadership. I'm writing part of this chapter while on leave. I'm eight weeks in and wow your body truly does keep score. The layers of literal shit my body has been through were heavy, painful, and impossible to ignore. I know we're not all in a position to take a leave and trust me I would have never done this by choice. But it's exactly what I needed.

The first two weeks I wept, I unraveled, I grieved the woman I was saying goodbye to. Then came the chronic pain. I was in and out of physio, chiro, massage, IMS needling. I had migraines, TMJ: the weight of the world on my shoulders. So much pain. I recall ugly crying on my husband's chest one night about how tired I was of the pressure I was putting on myself, the weight.

What would it feel like to let it go? To release myself from the urgency, the pressure, all of this shit I was putting on myself. It felt like I was sinking into the depths of the sea and I tied the weights on my feet myself. There had to be another way, and so there is. The weeping subsided, the chronic pain softened. I felt like I could breathe again, then entered exhaustion. My body was in fight or flight for so long as a warrior mama. I finally let the pressure go, and I needed rest, so much rest. Let this be your invitation too.

As I sit here on the eve of my forty-second birthday on a little solo writing retreat at a cottage ten minutes from my house, I realize all of it has been part of the healing, the shedding of the skin, the birth of a new identity. Because I'm an author now. I've always been a storyteller, and here we are.

### I SPENT NEARLY HALF MY LIFE BUILDING THIS IDENTITY, AND IT FELT LIKE IT WOULD ALL BE LOST.

That identity started slipping away the moment Goldie was born. I just didn't have the language for it yet. I held on to her like a toxic relationship. That corporate baddie was the final shedding of the skin of my past self. I was no longer her. The pain, the uncertainty, the trauma, the work, the gift of clarity had changed me. That woman was gone. I was just still holding her because I thought I needed to, because I was so scared to watch her sink into the sea.

Who would I be without her? Without the title, the

structure, the certainty? I'd be a mom to a sick kid. But several things can be true at the same time, can't they? I knew I was much more than that. I was a warrior, a quantum coach, a wild woman, a lover, a mom, an author, a runner, a friend, a sister, a daughter. I was much more than that. So are you, dear one. So are you.

Rewriting your identity doesn't happen all at once. It happens in micro-moments, like deciding to take a solo trip. Declaring you're an author before you publish your first book. Letting go of who you were and trusting who you're becoming.

The right things don't come from forcing. They come when you release what no longer fits. Releasing the labels that never truly belonged to you. The ones other people gave you. The ones the world whispered, or shouted, into your life before you ever had a chance to say who you really are.

No one's taught me that more than Goldie. From day one, people tried to define her: Palliative. Blind. Deaf. Brain stem dysfunction. Comfort care. Global developmental delays. Limits on what she'd do. Limits on who she'd become. Limits on how long she'd live, or whether she'd even matter.

I've had my own labels too: Caregiver. Warrior mom. Advocate. Too much. Not enough. Strong. Fragile. Capable. Overwhelmed.

Labels don't define you, unless you let them. Goldie never did. She has had more "fuck you, I'll do it anyway" moments than I can count. She has proved hundreds of specialists wrong. She has shattered every limit the world tried to put on her, just by existing. If she can do that... you sure as hell can shake off the labels that were never yours to carry.

You are not your diagnosis.

You are not your role.

You are not your past, your performance, your parenting, or your productivity.

You are *you.*

You get to make your own magic.

You are not a waste of space.

Neither is she.

Neither are we.

Shedding old skins is messy work. It isn't dramatic or clean. It doesn't happen all at once. It happens quietly, in the moments you realize a role no longer fits, a label feels heavy, a version of you has done her job and is ready to rest. There are women you've been who saved you. Women you had to become to survive certain seasons. Honouring them doesn't mean going backward. It means letting them soften their grip so something new can breathe.

Now, I'm going to go for a walk with all my selves, honouring each version of who I've been. I'll read through the journals from the last two years and relive the trauma, celebrate the wins. Goldie's first breath without oxygen support in the NICU. Passing her car seat challenge. The conversation with the neurologist that sent me spiralling into guilt and shame, and the car accident that followed on my way to the hospital. All of those women I've left behind are still in me. I am where I am today and who I am because of their sweat, their grit, their tears.

It's been hard to explain the energy it feels to relive those identities while writing this book and find gratitude and softness in it. To all that you are and all that you are becoming. Becoming isn't just an inner shift; it's a lived one. It starts to show up in how you move through the world, what you say yes to, and what you risk again after loss. For me, that proof came not in a journal entry or a ritual, but in something much more ordinary: our first family trip.

Understanding who I was becoming wasn't enough. I needed to see what it looked like in real life.

Our first family vacation as a family of four to Victoria, BC. It might sound small, a two-hour ferry ride and a few hours of driving, but for us, it was huge. Monumental, actually. Any kind of travel is complicated with Goldie. Packing isn't just clothes and snacks; it's:

1. Medical letters and emergency contacts
2. Medical equipment and backup chargers
3. Medications
4. Research on the nearest hospitals before we even book the hotel

It's not a trip, it's a mission. A military-grade operation disguised as a family getaway. No nurse. No backup support. Just Jeff, me, Frankie, and Goldie, figuring it out, one bag, one monitor, one deep breath at a time. We slept in one hotel room, taking turns staying awake, half-alert for alarms that never came. For most families, that's chaos. For us, it was heaven.

The moment I'll never forget was all four of us together

in the hotel pool. Goldie in our arms, kicking her tiny legs. Frankie squealing beside her, splashing us both. Jeff's eyes meeting mine, full of that wordless kind of joy, the kind that says, *We made it here.*

**THIS WASN'T JUST A VACATION. IT WAS PROOF.**

Proof that we could do hard things and still make them beautiful. Proof that our version of "normal" might look different, but it's still ours. Frankie has a hard time every time we go on a family trip and Goldie stays at Canuck Place for respite. She understands, but it still breaks her heart. This mattered.

Having Goldie there, swimming, playing, part of the world again, healed something in all of us. I was proud of us for making it happen. Proud of myself for even finding small moments within it, a short run, a few minutes in the sauna and steam room, a coffee I drank while it was hot. Little things that made me feel human again. It reminded me that joy and survival can coexist. That even inside the heaviness, life can still feel beautiful.

Something shifted that weekend. Somewhere between the ferry ride and the laughter in the pool, a new thought landed: If we can do this, what else might be possible? That question followed me home. It left me with the lingering sense that maybe there was room again for something that was just mine.

The thought alone felt rebellious, but also necessary. If not now, when? Magic doesn't always come from the easy chapters. Sometimes it's born in the exhaustion, the logistics, the hospital maps, and the half-packed medical bags. Sometimes, it's in the moment you look around, in a hotel pool, surrounded by love and realize, *this is what it means to be alive.*

That trip was our miracle, and it reminded me of something I'd forgotten for a long time: I still get to make my own magic.

A few weeks later, I found myself packing again, but this time, it wasn't suction machines or medical binders. It was notebooks, a tent, and courage. I was going on my first solo trip since Goldie was born. For two years, my identity had been tethered to survival, care schedules, medical updates, endless advocating. The idea of leaving, even for two days, felt impossible. Irresponsible, even. Something about that family trip made me think it was possible.

I booked the Women's Summit retreat. A weekend alone. No kids. No monitors. No one to take care of but me. I almost backed out ten times. Guilt is sneaky like that. It whispers, who are you to rest? Who are you to want more? But desire, the part of me that still believed in possibility, was louder. I went.

It wasn't glamorous. I didn't arrive "healed." I cried in the car halfway there. I almost turned around. But when I finally walked into that space surrounded by women who were also rewriting their lives, I exhaled for the first time in months. It felt like coming home to myself.

That weekend wasn't about "fixing" myself. It was about remembering who the fuck I was. I danced. I journaled. I sat in silence. I took long walks. I breathed.

Somewhere between the tears and the laughter, I

remembered the truth: I am still the wild woman, the storyteller. Magic isn't something you find. It's something you become. The family trip showed me what's possible when I let joy back in. The solo trip reminded me who I am when I do.

# YOUR 15-MINUTE RESET: IDENTITY IN MOTION

**Regulate:**

Find a quiet spot. Light a candle or simply place a hand on your heart. Let your breath slow down. This is a pause for you.

On a blank page, write down the identities, labels, or roles that no longer feel true.

"I'm always the one who…"
"I have to…"
"I can't because…"

These are the roles you learned to survive in — not the ones you're meant to live from now.

When you're done, circle the one that feels heaviest and whisper to yourself: "This is no longer mine to carry."

**Reflect:**

Now flip the script. Ask: *Who am I becoming?*

Write in present tense: "I am…"

Describe how she feels, moves, and speaks when she's not explaining herself.

Note what she's stopped tolerating, and what she's magnetizing instead.

Anchor into one micro-move you can take today that honours her.

**Reclaim:**
Close your eyes and step into the miracle mindset.

Imagine your Future Self walking into the room.

Notice her posture, energy, and presence.

Ask her: "What's one small way I can live you out loud today?"

Write down her answer. Then commit to doing it — even if it feels uncomfortable or unfinished.

*Mantra to close:* "I am not my past. I am not my labels. I am becoming, and that is magic."

# HOLD THE MIRACLE MINDSET

"You'll never find a rainbow
if you're looking down"

—CHARLIE CHAPLIN

I'VE ALWAYS LOVED RAINBOWS. WHO DOESN'T? THERE'S something magical about a kid chasing a rainbow, trying to find where it ends. Frankie has been chasing rainbows since she could walk. Unfortunately, rainbows took on another meaning after my first pregnancy loss. Rainbow baby. The hope of so many rainbow babies, and then finally, our little miracle Goldie was our rainbow baby.

Frankie wanted to name her Rainbow when she was born. For the first week or so, that's exactly what she called her. The name Goldie took a minute to grow on her, but she was obsessed with Goldie from the moment she met her. Doing hand hugs through the incubator, her little sister was covered in cords and a breathing tube. She kept waiting for her to get bigger and stronger to come home for months and never gave up faith. She is such a proud big sister. Watching her miracle mindset, and the connection her and Goldie have, is unbelievable.

Nowadays, Goldie is the most curious little sister, always eager to know what her big sister is up to. They have their own way to communicate, play, dance, sing. When Goldie is upset, we're talking meltdowns, which mean constant airway management, Frankie is the only one who can calm her down with a pat on her bum, a rub of her head, a whisper in her ear or a gentle lullaby. If I ever need a reminder of presence, gratitude and a miracle mindset, I look no further than my magical daughters. My greatest teachers. That's where the miracle mindset begins, with the faith of a child and the practice of a woman learning to remember it.

Watching Frankie's unwavering belief in her sister's

strength reminded me that miracles aren't rare. They are a way of seeing. That kind of faith, that quiet certainty in the impossible, is the foundation of the miracle mindset. Now that you're clear on who you're becoming, it's time to work on the mindset that aligns with that version of you. The miracle mindset is an essential part of stepping into your new story, your new identity, your new life, rewritten.

Watching Frankie love her sister so fiercely taught me something I didn't learn from books or quotes. A miracle mindset isn't about optimism; it's about staying open, especially when the outcome is uncertain.

As adults, faith looks different. It's not chasing rainbows anymore. It's choosing to move forward even when the answers don't exist yet.

An incredible lesson Goldie has taught me is to "keep them guessing." We joke a lot about our little "mystery girl" with a rare genetic disease so rare that she's still not diagnosed. She's taught me that you don't have to have the answers to begin. If we waited for answers before moving forward, we'd never move at all. What about the trust fall we've been told about? As Gabby Bernstein says in *The Universe Has Your Back,*

### "WHAT IF YOUR SUCCESS IS INEVITABLE?"

We've done a lot of waiting for answers with Goldie for tests, waiting for surgeries, waiting for treatments that might help. As a parent, knowing Goldie has an uncertain timeline, *like all of us*, waiting for answers isn't the energy I want to be in ever. But in a country with "free healthcare" like Canada, waitlists are normal. We've been unapologetically loud about waiting, about our nursing funding being cut, and about advocating for our girl. Unapologetic about it all.

Did I ever think I'd be on the news advocating for funding for our family and for others, for answers for rare genetic diseases when we hit dead ends? No. Did I reinvent myself because Goldie needed me to? Expand beyond my edges? Fuck yes. When the system is broken, it would be insane to stay quiet. So many people, especially women, stay dormant in their lives, dull their light, wake up thinking, well, this is it, I guess.

It's not.

Your wildest dreams are possible, so do something that scares you, be unapologetic in the reinvention of your life, your identity, because no one else is going to do it but you.

There's one moment that will forever define what the miracle mindset means to me. Goldie spent months in the NICU before she ever felt the sun or the sea. My only wish for my 40th birthday was to have her home, but that didn't happen. So, we brought the sea to her.

We decorated her hospital room with seashells and sea stones, small reminders of where she belonged. I worked with the hospital's spiritual support team to write a prayer for her healing, for peace, for one day by the water. The ocean has always been my reset, the place where I remember who I am. Its rhythm steadies me; its salt air clears the noise. I've always believed the sea holds a kind of ancient medicine, a memory older than words. Goldie, my little water sign, carries that same power. The same calm, ancient knowing. The same pull toward healing that the sea has always had for me.

A few weeks after she came home, we made that prayer real. We took her to the ocean and dipped her tiny toes into the waves. The air was warm, the light was gold, and for a brief, perfect moment, time stood still. The four of us together, laughing, alive. It was everything I'd wished for, just not how I expected it. When you're full of love, joy, and grounded certainty, even if nothing on the outside changes, something inside you already has.

You don't have to wait for a miracle. You can romanticize your life today. But here's the secret most people miss about miracles: They often start small. Living in the miracle mindset doesn't mean bypassing your pain or faking positivity. It means noticing the beauty that already exists and creating it on purpose, even in the smallest ways. I didn't call it anything at the time. I was just trying to find joy anywhere I could.

This is where the smallest things started to matter. Not as another thing to optimize. Not as a gratitude list I had to keep up with. But as moments. Small, sacred interruptions that soften your nervous system and remind you that life isn't only effort and endurance.

Sometimes it's a perfectly made coffee, a song that hits at the right moment.

Sometimes it's light through the trees when you least expect it.

Tiny Joys don't change your circumstances. They change

how it feels to live inside them. My body didn't care about mindset. It responded to relief. It learned:

We're safe.
We're allowed to feel good.
This moment doesn't have to be rushed through.

That's where miracles take root.

**Regulate:**

Pick one part of your day that usually feels automatic or draining.
The commute. The morning chaos. The dishes at night.

Before you change anything, pause.
Take one slow breath.
Unclench your jaw. Drop your shoulders.

You're not trying to feel good yet.
You're just letting your nervous system stand down.

**Reflect:**

Notice how you're moving through this moment.

Are you rushing it?
Checking out?
Bracing for what comes next?

Ask yourself, honestly: What would make this moment easier to be in?

Not better.
Not productive.

Just less tight.

This is where the miracle mindset begins.
Not with positivity.
With presence.

**Reclaim:**
Make one small adjustment.

Light a candle while you fold the laundry.
Put on music you like on the walk to daycare.
Drink your coffee while it's hot instead of standing at the counter scrolling.
Add lemon to your water because you can.

Then ask: What's one small way I can support myself in this moment?

Do that.
Tiny joys don't change your circumstances. They change your experience of them.
And when life is unpredictable, that matters.

We are never truly out of the woods, so maybe it's time to stop rushing through them.

# THE RISE

---

*Part III*

# LEAD WITH THE GOLDIE EFFECT

"You are the sky. Everything else, it's just the weather."

—PEMA CHÖDRÖN

**YOU DON'T REWRITE YOUR LIFE JUST FOR YOU.**

You rewrite it for your kids who are watching.

For your partner who needs your truth more than your perfection.

For your friends who are quietly waiting for permission to do the same.

That's the Goldie Effect.

One small shift. One tiny act of courage. One whispered yes. Then suddenly, the ripple moves through everyone around you. It's about living your rewrite in real time, showing up as future you now, and letting the world rearrange itself in response.

Ripples often carry us to places we could never have planned. The courage to take one small step, to say one quiet yes, opens the door for synchronicities, support, and solutions you couldn't have scripted.

Remember the story of how we found ABM? Through a healer's cousin. A miracle daughter. A voice note thread that became a lifeline. That's the kind of magic I'm talking about here. You don't have to know how it will unfold. You just have to trust that there's more available than what you can currently see.

We don't always know how the miracles will arrive, but we do know the small choices that make us ready for them. Magic doesn't just appear; it shows up in the tiny decisions we make every day. Life isn't one giant turning point: it's a series of tiny ones. You don't wake up one day in a life you don't recognize.

You build it through compromises, choices, and the small moments you didn't think mattered. If you want to rewrite your life, you don't start with a grand plan. You start with fifteen minutes. You start with one micro-move.

You start with the next right decision. Every small choice becomes part of the map to the life you actually want. Not the life you tolerated. Not the one you inherited, but the one you're building on purpose. When your body starts to rush, that's the moment to pause.

That's the miracle mindset. It's not delusion, it's devotion. Devotion to the version of you that believes life can feel better, that your story isn't over. It's never too late to start again. But embodying the rewrite isn't glamorous. It's gritty. It lives in the mornings when your nervous system wants to sprint before sunrise.

Sometimes, those tiny decisions reveal how close we've been to the edge, how even one millimetre can hold the weight of a whole life. I got the call after my surgery. They'd removed all the cancer, but the margins weren't what they wanted. One millimetre short. Medically, it didn't mean much for this type of cancer. But emotionally, it hit like a landslide. It felt like a metaphor for everything I'd been holding, how close I'd been to collapse without realizing it. How one millimetre can be the difference between "you're fine" and "you need more surgery." How invisible thresholds can carry such enormous weight.

Embodying the rewrite isn't elegant or optimized. It happens inside real mornings, real pressure, and real lives that don't pause just because you've had a breakthrough. That one millimetre taught me something: You can do everything "right" and still not feel safe. You can check every box and still be asked to wait. You can lead others and still be terrified, sitting in the unknown. Even one millimetre of movement, one millimetre of release, of truth, of courage, is enough to change your life.

Over time, that lesson deepened into something bigger than us, bigger than medicine, bigger than one family's fight to survive. Somewhere along this journey, I came across a phrase that stopped me cold. In Italy, they don't say special needs. They say special rights. That small shift in language hit like a lightning bolt. It reframed everything we'd been fighting for, from pity to power, from "extra help" to inherent belonging, because access isn't charity. Support isn't a favour: they're rights.

For years, I'd been conditioned to explain, to justify, to prove why Goldie deserved the same care, safety, and presence as anyone else. But special rights flipped the script. Goldie doesn't live outside the system; she reveals where it needs to evolve. She isn't an exception. She's an invitation to rethink care, to widen compassion. To remember what community means.

That's the deeper pulse of The Goldie Effect.

It's not inspiration or charity, it's reclamation. It's building a world where care is a collective rhythm, not an individual burden. Where families like ours aren't just surviving inside the cracks, we're leading the rebuild. That lesson, that one millimetre can change everything, isn't just about medicine. It's about life itself: the moments when you're holding it all together, and reality still crashes in anyway.

Writing your dream life down is easy. Living it out loud? That's where it gets real. I came home from my writing retreat glowing with purpose, excited to keep going. Within thirty-six hours, chaos ensued:

Goldie was spiking a fever. Possible emergency.
My husband was holding it together by a
single nerve.
Frankie was melting down, running away
from school.
I was... exhausted.

It made me ask the question I know you've probably whispered, too: How the hell do I rewrite my life when I barely have thirty seconds to myself? Not with high vibes and vision boards (though I love those too), but with the scrappy, gritty, heart-led decision to keep going even when it's hard.

To get up early. To take the five minutes in the bathroom before the baby wakes. To protect your peace like it's sacred, because it is. You're allowed to fall apart. You're allowed to take turns holding it all. My husband and I have done that more times than I can count. One of us shatters, the other holds. Then we switch.

That's the dance of the rewrite. The sacred mess. The rhythm of rising. Those stolen moments of stillness, those two-minute breathers, those fifteen-minute rewrites, are everything. They're the bridge between who you are and who you're becoming. They're the moments that expand your capacity for more.

Leadership isn't forged in perfect conditions. It's revealed when everything feels like too much. When time is scarce, and pressure is loud. In those moments, the work isn't control; it's boundaries. It's energy. It's choosing, again and again, what gets access to your inner world. You don't need more time. You need presence. Even a few minutes of devotion to who you're becoming is enough to shift the moment and yourself with it.

Early in this book, in chapter three, I discussed owning your energy and a dream of confronting a family member. Less than a month after I had that dream, it came true. I was faced with this hard conversation about them coming for a visit, and how draining it felt for me. It was heartbreaking and painful to set new boundaries with my family but I had to share my truth and invite them along the journey.

Identity-level change sometimes means leaving people behind. You can have the hard conversations. You can invite people to expand with you. But sometimes you have to accept that not everyone will come. That loss can feel devastating.

For me, it meant expecting more from the people around our family. We had to level up, and I needed everyone in our inner circle to meet us there. If they couldn't, I had to let that be okay.

I told my family that we needed to be surrounded by people who believed Goldie is a miracle, not people who felt sorry for us. Even love, when it's soaked in fear, can be too heavy.

We can't control how the world reacts to Goldie, but we can choose who we let into our home and into our inner circle. Only love. Only light. Only joy. Goldie is sensitive to the energy around her, and we want her life to feel like love for every second she's here.

I didn't expect it, but that conversation forced something open in me. It felt like grief and freedom at the same time. When I stopped trying to manage everyone else's emotions, I finally understood that my responsibility was to stay in my own lane. Not everyone else's healing.

It didn't go well. It was heartbreaking. But I did the hard thing. The conversation went worse than I imagined, and I survived. I felt free.

And something unexpected happened. My family rose. They came with us.

That's what stepping into a new identity does. It asks you to tell the truth, even when it costs you something. And once you do, the fear that kept you stuck starts to loosen its grip.

**I woke up the next morning asking myself:**
What am I still afraid of?
Why am I not launching the course?
Why am I still stuck in a job that's not aligned?
Why am I waiting to be her, the future version of me I already know is possible?

I already did the scariest thing I could imagine, and I'm still here. That's when I realized the shift never starts with confidence. It starts with trust. Self-trust isn't loud. It shows up before the evidence does. It's choosing what's right for you, even when no one else understands it yet. Self-leadership comes next. It's standing in what you believe. It's doing what needs to be done, not for applause, but because your future self is counting on you.

It doesn't always look like action. Sometimes it looks like rest. Sometimes it sounds like silence. You can lead in the quiet. You can lead in the loud. Either way, you are leading.

**SELF-TRUST IS TAKING THE STEP. SELF-LEADERSHIP IS STAYING WITH IT. SURRENDER IS TRUSTING THE GROUND WILL HOLD, EVEN WHEN YOU CAN'T SEE THE WHOLE PATH YET.**

Stop waiting for the "perfect time" to start. Life isn't going to suddenly slow down and hand you space. You don't need more time. You need permission. Start before you feel ready. Start messy. Small, imperfect action is what changes things

If I had to distill everything I've learned about changing a life that feels too full, too heavy, or too loud, it would come down to this: small, intentional blocks of time, practiced consistently.

Nothing meaningful in our life changed through force or urgency. Not Goldie's healing. Not my capacity. Not this book. Every real shift came through gentle, connected steps. One brave move at a time.

The 15-Minute Rewrite is the practice.

The Goldie Effect is what happens when you live it.

# YOUR 15-MINUTE RESET: THE GOLDIE EFFECT IN ACTION

**Regulate:**

Sit.

Breathe.

Let your body soften just enough to stand down from urgency.

You're not here to breakthrough.

You're here to arrive.

Imagine a one-millimetre shift.

Unclench your jaw.

Drop your shoulders.

Release the pressure to fix everything all at once. This work doesn't respond to force.

**Reflect:**

Journal on one question only: Where am I holding back because the move feels too small to matter?

Don't expand it.

Don't justify it.

Just tell the truth.

**Reclaim:**
Take one tiny action that aligns with who you're becoming.

Send the message.
Protect the time.
Say the honest thing.
Stop waiting for the moment to feel bigger.

Then remind yourself:

I don't need the red carpet.
I don't need permission.
I don't need certainty.

My micro-moves are how I lead now.

# LIVE IT OUT LOUD

"Do the earth a favor:
Don't hide your magic."

—YUNG PUEBLO

**HERE'S WHAT NO ONE TELLS YOU ABOUT HAVING A CHILD** with complex medical needs: the world starts measuring them. Milestones. Progress charts. Percentiles. Without realizing it, you start measuring yourself too.

I felt like I was failing. But Goldie never cared about the chart. She taught me that life isn't about hitting the "right" milestones at the "right" time, it's about squeezing every last drop out of the moments you do get, even if they look nothing like you pictured. That's the heartbeat of how we live now.

I've been gentle with myself and with others. Trying to keep the spark lit. Trying to live what I now know. Because real presence isn't just found in a weekend; it's found in the rituals you build when you get home. In the way you keep choosing yourself, day after day. For me, choosing myself became a revolution that didn't look loud, but wasn't passive either. For years now, my husband and I have had a quiet ritual we return to every year. We sit down together and name our goals. Not in a flashy way. Not in a vision-board, manifest-and-forget kind of way. We write them down. We revisit them. We talk about what they'll require. On average, we hit about eighty percent of them.

One of the areas we always return to is our family, and since Goldie was born, that has meant setting goals that don't look anything like the ones we used to write. Not promotions or trips or timelines, but outcomes that would give her more comfort, more capacity, more life.

There were three big ones.

The first was moving Goldie from being fed into her

small intestine to being fed through her stomach. We believed her body could tolerate it, that it would help with digestion and reflux. That it would give us the option to feed her real food, not just broken-down formula. That it would free her from being attached to tubing for eighteen hours a day, always tethered, always limited. Being able to pick her up, move with her, be close to her, matters more than I can explain.

The second was getting her off seizure medication. This one took us a long time. The only documented seizures Goldie ever had been in her first days of life, when she was born premature at thirty-three weeks. Still, she was placed on heavy seizure meds early on, and the dosage was increased as time went on, based on symptoms that we later learned weren't seizures at all, but something else entirely. These medications can be lifesaving when they're needed, but when they're not, they can slow development, cause sedation, and mask what's possible. We pushed gently at first, then more firmly. EEGs. MRIs. Conversations that took months. It took a long time for neurology to feel comfortable, but eventually, test after test showed no seizure activity, they agreed to a conservative wean. By early 2026, Goldie will be off seizure medication entirely. That alone feels monumental.

The third goal was the hardest to name out loud: finding a diagnosis or a treatment for Goldie. Something, anything. We had exhausted everything available to us in Canada, and much of what was available in the U.S. too. Then we learned about a new team out of Harvard working with RNA sequencing, using technology that isn't widely accessible yet, combined with AI, to fill in genetic gaps that traditional testing can't reach. The cost was staggering. Fifteen thousand U.S. dollars, and there were no guarantees.

But we kept going.

As of this December, Goldie was approved to be part of a pilot program at our local hospital. The second pilot of its kind in all of Canada. Goldie will be the child in that pilot. By the time this book is in your hands, we will have started.

None of this happened quietly.

There was nothing passive about these goals. They didn't come from hoping harder or waiting patiently or trusting that things would sort themselves out. Every single one of them required advocacy. Meetings. Emails. Follow-ups. Feeding teams. Neurology. Genetics. Respirology. Pediatricians. Dietitians. Endless conversations. Second opinions. Standing in rooms and staying there when it would have been easier to walk away.

Some doors only opened because we stood in front of them long enough. There were moments when it felt easier to stop asking, to accept the version of reality we were being handed. But that was never really an option. Goldie needed us present. Vocal, in the room, repeatedly.

Believing something is possible doesn't absolve you from work. It means you stay engaged long after it would be reasonable to give up. I'm sharing this not because these goals are universal. They aren't. Yours will look different. I'm sharing it because all three of them have either happened or are actively unfolding right now, and that still takes my breath away.

Not because it was easy.

Not because it was graceful.

But because it was real.

This is what living out loud has looked like for us. Naming what matters. Staying in it. Advocating without apology. Refusing to disappear just because the system is slow or loud or uncertain. And if there's anything I know for sure now, it's this: expansion doesn't come from wishing. It comes from participation. From showing up. From choosing, repeatedly, to believe something is possible and then staying long enough to help make it real. I used to say goodnight to Goldie like it might be the last time.

I'd hold her close, breathe her in, study every inch of her. Her skin. Her breath. Her weight in my arms. I would tell her I loved her in that way you do when you don't know if you'll see someone again. I'm not sure when it changed. There was no moment, no announcement. Somewhere along the way, I stopped saying goodnight like that. Now I say it the way a mother says it when she knows she'll see her child in the morning.

"Have good dreams. I love you."

The reality is, she's more resilient now, and so am I.

This book isn't a finish line. It's a way of living. One that says you don't need to blow up your life to begin again. You need truth, love, and fifteen minutes a day. You're not late. This is your rewrite.

Earlier in this book, I mentioned the green, glass-clear lake on Cortes Island.

The place I went to feel held.

For a long time, I thought I needed to go back there to remember how to listen to myself.

Somewhere along the way, I realized I didn't.

I learned how to go inward without disappearing.

How to trust what surfaced when everything went quiet.

I carry that with me now.

It shows up in a breath between tasks.

In a walk at dawn.

In the way I stay present when things get hard.

Nothing about our life has been linear. Healing included. There are ups and downs, ebbs and flows, spirals and plot twists. Rolling with it, being adaptable, isn't just a survival skill; it's a path to joy.

You don't have to carry every event like it defines you.

Just because something cracked you open doesn't mean it broke you. Maybe it made space for the miracle.

That's not linear. That's boundless.

# AFTERWORD

YOU DIDN'T COME HERE TO BURN YOUR LIFE DOWN. YOU came because something in you knew there had to be another way to live without losing yourself in the process.

The fire was real. It cracked things open you couldn't ignore anymore, even the parts you would have preferred to keep sealed shut. It asked for your attention. It demanded honesty. For a while, it felt like survival was the whole story. But the work was never about staying there.

It wasn't about reliving it or proving what you endured. The rewrite was quieter than that. It was learning how to stay with yourself once everything was exposed. Learning how to regulate when your body wanted to run. How to tell the truth without handing it over. How to choose differently, not all at once, but small moments that held.

Somewhere in that process, something else became clear.

Not everything needs to be shared.

Not everything needs to be explained.

Not everything is meant to be touched by everyone.

Some things are meant to be protected.

That's the vault.

The place where you keep what matters most once you finally recognize its value.

Your energy. Your truth. Your tenderness.

The parts of you that are no longer available for debate, fixing, or public consumption.

The rise isn't a finish line. It's what happens when you start living from that protected place. When your nervous system softens because it finally knows what's safe to hold and what no longer gets access. When your life gets quieter, truer, and more yours.

This is how you rewrite your life without burning it all down.

You don't disappear.

You don't detonate.

You don't give everything away.

You keep what's sacred close.

And you lead from there.

# KEEP REWRITING

WHEN YOU ZOOM OUT, YOUR LIFE STARTS TO LOOK LIKE a movie timeline. Plot twists. Low points. Miracles. Lessons you didn't ask for but carry anyway. The dips weren't detours. They were rewrites in disguise.

## CREATE YOUR OWN REWRITE MAP

Draw a simple timeline of your life so far.

Mark the moments that changed you, and the insights that came after.

Then gently ask yourself: If nothing changed, what would my life look like six months from now? And if everything did?

This is about paying attention.

## A FEW BRAVE MOVES THAT KEEP THE REWRITE ALIVE

The Goldie Effect isn't one moment. It's a series of small, steady choices that quietly change everything. This isn't a checklist. It's a reflection of what's already underway.

**Let yourself want more.** Not because you're ungrateful, but because something in you knows there's more life available than the one you've been living.

**Reclaim who you are.** You are not your diagnosis, your role, your productivity, or the version of you that survived something hard.

**Let your stories refine you, not define you.** What you've lived through matters. It just doesn't get the final word.

**Allow grace in the plot twist.** Some detours aren't mistakes. They're invitations you couldn't have planned for.

**Release what no longer fits.** People. Patterns. Dreams that belonged to an earlier version of you. Outgrowing things is not failure.

**Take one honest step.** Change doesn't come from knowing. It comes from doing.

**Let it be easier than you think.** Support isn't weakness. Rest isn't quitting. Spaciousness doesn't come after the work. It is the work.

You've already paused. You've already gotten clearer. You've already made aligned moves and stepped into the magnetism of who you really are. You've walked through the fire. Now you get to keep rewriting, one day at a time.

**Journal Prompt:** One year from now, I will thank myself for...

# A FEW WORDS WE COME BACK TO

THESE ARE WORDS THAT KEPT SHOWING UP AS I WROTE this book. Not because I planned them, but because they were already doing the work. They're not here to explain anything. They're touchstones. Language that helps orient you when things feel unclear. Words you may recognize before you fully understand them.

## THE GOLDIE EFFECT™

The quiet shift that happens when life changes you and you choose to respond with presence instead of panic.

## THE 15-MINUTE REWRITE™

A simple practice for real life. You give yourself fifteen minutes to come back into your body, tell yourself the truth, and take one aligned step forward. Not to fix everything, just to stay with yourself.

# REGULATE · REFLECT · RECLAIM

The rhythm of the work.
**Regulate:** settle your nervous system enough to feel safe again.
**Reflect:** get honest about what's true.
**Reclaim:** choose one small action that supports who you're becoming.

## MICRO-MOMENTS

Small pockets of intention that change things. A pause. A breath. A decision. This is where transformation lives. Not in big declarations.

## CAPACITY

Your emotional, physical, and energetic bandwidth on any given day. Capacity isn't fixed. It expands and contracts. Learning to respect it is how you stop burning yourself out.

## ANCHOR PRACTICES

Simple grounding rituals that bring you back to yourself. Breathing. Movement. Writing. Stepping outside. They don't need to be fancy to be effective.

## IDENTITY REWRITING

The process of loosening old roles and stories and choosing who you are now. It happens slowly, through repetition and self-trust, not force.

## PLOT TWIST

An unexpected moment that reroutes your life. Often uncomfortable. Often clarifying. Not a mistake, but a turning point.

## REWIRING

Changing a pattern that no longer serves you. Not by pretending everything is fine, but by choosing a different response when it matters most.

## EMBODIMENT

Letting what you know show up in how you live. When insight moves out of your head and into your body, your choices start to change.

## PARTS WORK

The practice of listening to the different parts of you without letting any one of them take over. The scared part. The angry part. The protector. The one just trying to get through the day. None of them are wrong. They're all trying to help.

## MIRACLE MINDSET

Staying open when outcomes are uncertain.
Not blind optimism, but a willingness to remain present and engaged long enough for something meaningful to emerge, even when the path isn't visible yet.

## THE VAULT

The inner place where you keep what's sacred. Your energy. Your truth. Your tenderness. Not everything belongs in the open. Some things are meant to be protected.

# THE REWRITE MAP

*A WAY TO CHOOSE THE RIGHT 15-MINUTE REWRITE BASED* on *what your nervous system needs right now.*

Use this when you're overwhelmed, stuck, or unsure where to begin.

Start with the feeling. The right entry point will reveal itself.

## WHEN YOU FEEL OVERSTIMULATED, SCATTERED, OR EMOTIONALLY FRIED

Your system needs grounding before insight.

→ **Own Your Energy: The Energy Audit**

Helps you identify what's draining you, what's restoring you, and make one clean, energetic decision instead of spiralling. Page: 84

→ **Hold the Miracle Mindset: Tiny Joys**

Brings your nervous system out of survival and back into presence through small sensory shifts. Page: 164

## WHEN YOU FEEL STUCK IN A LOOP YOU CAN'T SEEM TO BREAK

Your system is protecting you, not sabotaging you.

→ **Clear the Sh*t That's Blocking You: The Block Breaker**

Lets the scared part speak, understand what it's protecting, and soften the block instead of fighting it. Page: 107

→ **Get Ruthless About What You Really Want: The Belief Bridge**

Builds a bridge between fear and action by naming the story that's running the show and choosing one honest move. Page: 128

## WHEN YOU FEEL EMOTIONALLY HEAVY, NUMB, OR DISCONNECTED FROM YOUR BODY

Your system needs safety, not answers.

→ **Heal What You've Been Avoiding: Let the Body Lead**

Moves you out of your head and back into your body through sensation, music, and gentle awareness. Page: 140

**→ Go Inward: The Inward Adventure**

Helps you turn inward without collapsing, and invest in your own regulation, peace, and healing. Page: 117

## WHEN LIFE HAS THROWN YOU A CURVEBALL YOU DIDN'T PLAN FOR

Your system needs steadiness, not control.

**→ Navigate Plot Twists:  Holding Grace in Chaos**

Supports you in naming what you're navigating and choosing who you want to be inside the chaos. Page: 95

## WHEN YOU FEEL READY TO MOVE, BUT HESITANT TO LEAD

Your system needs permission and momentum.

**→ Make Your Own Magic: Identity in Motion**

Helps you release outdated identities and step into who you're becoming, one embodied micro-move at a time. Page: 155

→ **Lead with the Goldie Effect: The Goldie Effect in Action**

Anchors leadership through micro-actions, not grand ges-
tures. This is embodiment, not performance. Page: 178

# AUTHOR'S NOTE

IF YOU'VE REACHED THIS PAGE, YOU'VE ALREADY REWRITTEN something: the way you see yourself. When I began this book, I thought I was telling my daughter's story. Somewhere along the way, I realized I was also telling yours and mine. Goldie taught me that miracles don't always roar. Sometimes they whisper, *keep going.*

Wherever you are on your own timeline, remember this: you are proof that light returns.  Keep choosing softness. Presence. Love. Even when the world asks for something harder. This is the Goldie Effect in motion.

Thank you for walking this path with me.

Forever cheering you on,
**Michelle**

# ABOUT THE AUTHOR

**AFTER YEARS IN CORPORATE LEADERSHIP, MICHELLE** Hooey's life shifted with the birth of her second daughter, Goldie, who was born with complex medical needs in 2023. What followed wasn't a reinvention. It was a reckoning with capacity, identity, grief, love, and what it means to stay present when life no longer follows the plan. Out of that season came The Goldie Effect and the 15-Minute Rewrite. A simple, embodied framework for change rooted in regulation, truth, and small, honest action.

Michelle's work sits at the intersection of lived experience and practical transformation. She writes and speaks about navigating uncertainty, protecting energy, and building lives that can actually be lived. Especially for parents, caregivers, and people in the thick of real change.

Michelle lives in Vancouver, British Columbia with Jeff, their daughters Frankie and Goldie, and two Labradoodles, Soda and Artie.

You can learn more at anchorlesscoaching.com or follow her on Instagram @michelle_hooey.

# ACKNOWLEDGEMENTS

**TO EVERYONE WHO HAS SUPPORTED OUR FAMILY OVER** the last three years. Cheering Goldie on has brought light into some of our darkest days. We felt it. We still do.

To you, the reader, for taking a chance on this book, and on me. Thank you for being here.

To my husband, Jeff, my hunk daddy and my anchor. Thank you for holding my hand through the hardest days of my life, for making me laugh when things felt unbearable, and for giving me the space and encouragement to keep going when I wanted to give up on this book.

To my mentor, Megan Reed. Thank you for creating a space where I could be held through the life-shattering experience of writing this book. I would not have finished without you.

To my incredible editor, Alethea, for your wisdom, steadiness, and sharp eye. This book is stronger because of you.

To Taryn, for your design work, and to Elle, for the beautiful book cover that holds this story so well.

To all my early readers, thank you for your care, honesty, and belief in this work from the very beginning.

To my parents, for always being there, and for your love, steadiness, and unwavering support. To my sister, Lyndsey, for being the very best.

To my Norgren family, for being in the trenches with

us day after day, month after month. I am so lucky to call you family.

Sandra, I don't have words big enough to describe how your relentless support has changed everything for our family. We would not still be standing without you.

To the many caregivers, nurses, and quiet helpers who showed up along the way, thank you.

My girls, Frankie and Goldie, my greatest teachers. You have expanded my capacity for love, presence, and wonder.

They say being in a room with powerful people expands you, and it does. I'm endlessly grateful for the Vancouver women entrepreneur community, for the brilliance, courage, and ambition that lives there. I'm grateful, too, for the global community of quantum coaches who held me, challenged me, and walked beside me, especially you, Ashley Gordon.

But nothing has expanded me the way being in a room with my girls has. To sit with children who are fully embodied and wildly alive. To watch them navigate their bodies and this world with fearlessness, curiosity, and love feels like the greatest education of my life.

You are the light that guides me. I will forever be grateful that you chose me as your mom.

Go, Goldie, go.